Back to the Beginning

My Journey of Faith, Pain and Blessings

Lauretta L. Hall Thrist

Copyright © 2015 Lauretta L. Hall Thrist
All rights reserved
First Edition

PAGE PUBLISHING, INC.
New York, NY

First originally published by Page Publishing, Inc. 2015

ISBN 978-1-68139-414-5 (pbk)
ISBN 978-1-68139-415-2 (digital)

Printed in the United States of America

Dedication

This book is dedicated to anyone that has suffered under the control of someone else. I would also like to dedicate this book to my grandchildren; Malika, Myles, Naya, Toni, and the twins; Langston and Landen, and my youngest grandchild; Layla. Also, to my newly added grandchildren; Jabari and Shade', and my great-grandchildren; Lavante, Jahlani, and Zariah. I treasure each and every one of you and thank God for the constant joy that you bring into our lives.

Acknowledgements

First I want to thank my Heavenly Father for giving me the strength and the courage to write this book. I would like to thank my oldest son Alton for giving up a lot of your childhood to help me raise your sister's. You will never know how much I appreciate you. I want to thank my middle son Tony for encouraging words, checking on the progress of my book and for being the best parts of his father. I want to thank my oldest daughter Emtesha for her support and suggestions, I have learned so much from you, I treasure your friendship. I want to thank my youngest daughter Mela'nie for being supportive and strong in spite of the many obstacles she has faced in her short life, Mela'nie you are my hero. I want to acknowledge my youngest son; Oliver Caleb for showing me that I had room in my heart for another child. I didn't give birth to you, but I love you as if I did. And, last but never least I thank my husband Oliver for his constant words of encouragement, support and love. You are the wind beneath my wings and I love you more than words can express. I would be remiss in not thanking Charisse and my other siblings, and my other relatives and friends for your support and encouragement. Also, a special thank you to my daughter-in-laws; Kristal and Tequila and my son-in-law Charles for their encouragement and support.

One

My name is Lauretta Louise Hall Shelvin Hughes Thrist. As you read my autobiography, you will realize why I have so many last names! However, I can explain my first and middle names. My father's mother's name was Laura Weiss before she married my grandfather Henry. Grandmother Laura died when my father was only twelve years old. All I know about her was that she was part Choctaw Indian and had very long hair, and the most important thing is that I looked just like her; therefore I inherited her name. My middle name was for my other grandmother Louise Rogers Shannon. "Laura Louise"—really, are you kidding me? My parents had pity on me and changed the *Laura* to *Lauretta*; if they hadn't, I would have found a way to do it myself.

My parents were from the South, and like so many other African American families, they moved up North to find employment and a better life. My father was from Red Banks, Mississippi, (please don't ask me where Red Banks is because I really have no clue). My mother was born in Toledo, Ohio, and lived there a couple of months before my grandparents moved back to Memphis, Tennessee, where the rest of my mother's family lived. As far as I know, my mother was the only one who was born outside Memphis. I think my grandparents went to Ohio to seek their fortune, and when it didn't work out, they returned to where the rest of the family lived.

My parents were secretly married when she was around nineteen years old. Maybe I should explain why their marriage was a secret. My mother dated my father against my grandparents' wishes. You see, back in those days, African Americans were prejudice toward each other (some still are)! I believe it derived from the slave mentality that developed when my ancestors were slaves. The light-skinned slaves were always chosen to work in masa's house, while the darker slaves were sent to the fields to pick cotton or whatever type of food they grew on the plantation. And instead of ending that type of thinking when slavery was over, many African Americans continued thinking that being light was being right! People went so far as to judge a person's color by a brown paper bag! If you were lighter than the bag, then you were considered light and right; if not, you were often described as "sambo" or other unattractive names. Well, my father was a very dark-skinned, handsome man that certainly didn't meet my grandparents' standards.

I remember my aunt telling me that my parents were married with only my mother's brother Charles and his wife, Pearline, in attendance. My mother was so afraid of what my grandparents would do that after the wedding she returned home and acted as if nothing had changed! It surprised me that my father went along with that arrangement, but he must have been head over heels in love to agree to spend his honeymoon alone! When my grandparents found out my parents were married, they sent my mother to New York to live with her sister, my aunt LaRaine. Eventually my father went to New York to claim his bride, and they eventually moved to Rockford, Illinois, the so-called land of opportunity!

My father, Eddie Hall, was an awesome body-and-fender man and taught his trade to others when he lived in Memphis. My father was also very handy with his hands, he could do construction work and electrical (this proved pretty handy when they purchased their first fixer-upper home). When they moved to Rockford, my father worked at a body-and-fender shop with his friend Roy Sims until he was able to open his own shop. Mr. Sims worked on the inside of cars, and my father took care of the outside. Evidently everything went well for a while until they decided to end the partnership. I was never given a reason for the abrupt separation.

My mother, Marion Louise Shannon Hall, attended Lemoyne-Owens College in Memphis, Tennessee, for two years, and while she received her associates in education, she also became a member of the Delta Sigma Theta Sorority Inc. Mama came from a long line of teachers, including some of her aunts and her mother. My mother was also a pianist and had the distinct honor of becoming one of the musicians at Trinity Methodist Church when she was just twelve years old. When my parents moved to Rockford, my mother worked at William Dennis Elementary School in Rockford, Illinois, as a special education teacher.

My parents brought a small house that my father completely remodeled, and they both became members of our family church, Providence Missionary Baptist, where my mother played the piano for the Angelic Choir. And as a matter of fact, my father's parents were charter members of Providence. My father joined the senior choir and became a mentor to some of the younger men at the church; one of his favorites, Willie James Howard, later became a deacon and choir member.

Two

From all accounts they were a very happy couple and were excited to welcome their first child in July 1949. My mother said that Beverly was very spoiled being the first child, so much so that often my father had to take her for a ride in the car to get her to sleep. In November 1950 my brother Melvin was born. He was my mother's pride and joy. You see, my grandmother put her sons on pedestals, and when Melvin was born, my mother did the same thing. Melvin was what Beverly and I referred to as a bookworm; I don't remember a time that Melvin didn't have his nose stuck in a book. He wore glasses, so he looked like a little professor instead of a regular brother.

My father became very ill after Melvin was born and ended up in Edward Heinz Jr. VA Hospital in Chicago, Illinois. My father was so ill that the doctor called my mother and told her to come to the hospital because my father was gravely ill, and they did not think he would make it through the night. My mother and my aunt Carrie V prayed all the way to the hospital, and when they arrived, my father was sitting up in the bed talking. He asked why my mother had left Rockford and come over in the middle of the night to Chicago to see him. Needless to say, the doctors didn't have the final say regarding my father. My mother was cautioned against getting pregnant because Daddy's illness could cause serious sinus problems for any child that she became pregnant with. My mother's physician, Dr. Roberts, gave my mother shots to keep her from getting pregnant. Surprise, surprise, the shots didn't work because here I am!

The first thing I remember was hearing my mother say, "You weren't supposed to be here." Now that statement can be taken a number of ways; however, none of them sounded good! I was the third child of a total of five children born to my mother. The three older children are eighteen months apart. As I mentioned earlier, my older sister, Beverly, was born in July 1949, my brother Melvin was born in November 1950, and I was born in April 1952. I was a very active child from the beginning, my mother nicknamed me Twisty Bottom. She said that whenever she tried to change my diaper, I would start twisting around and would not keep still. I figured it was my natural dancing talent that was being revealed! From what I was told, I was a very happy baby until I started getting my hair done!

When I was born, I had a head full of thick, coarse hair. And, to my mother's dismay, I was extremely tinder headed, my head hurt when it was combed (for those of you reading this book who may not be familiar with this terminology). It hurt so bad that I literally got sick when I realized it was "the day" for me to get my hair washed and braided. I didn't mind getting my hair washed or even getting it braided; however, it was the time between that made me want to take a hit out on my mother! I vividly remember sitting between her legs on the floor and feeling like I wanted to die; she was hurting me so bad! I cried, ran a fever, and got a headache each time I had to go through the ordeal. My mother used to compare my hair to a spring. Yeah, you read right—a spring. She went on to say that as soon as she was able to comb through my hair, the waves in my hair would make my hair spring back, and it would tangle again! I couldn't believe she had the nerve to complain to her friends about my hair when I was the one on the receiving end of the pain. I often found myself praying for thinner hair like Beverly's or shorter hair like Melvin's.

Three

In 1957 I found out some very disturbing news, news that a five-year-old should never have to hear: You are no longer the baby of the house! Now at five I was old enough to realize that Mama was getting bigger, but I must have rationalized it was because she really liked eating her cooking! Then I remember my mother had to go to the hospital for a few days, and I thought she had eaten so much that she burst open, and they had to sew her back together. Well, it made sense to me! I remember the day she came home with my little sister Charisse, the first thing I noticed was that she was pretty, had "good hair," and, most of all, that she had light skin! She was the first one in our family who had light skin, and I hated her! Maybe I shouldn't say *hate*, it's such a strong word, but I didn't like her and wondered why she was there. I remember telling my parents that they should just take her back, we had enough kids, and maybe she could be someone else's baby.

In looking back to my first thoughts of Charisse, it explains the many fights we had when we were kids. Charisse was very different from my sister Beverly and I; she didn't like the same things we did. I remember my mother putting this pretty yellow dress on Charisse; it was embroidered with little white and yellow flowers around the hem of the dress, and it stood out when she put on her petty coat. We told her to turn around and see how pretty the dress would look in the mirror. Charisse looked at me and Mama like we were crazy and tried to tear the dress so she could take it off! Charisse wanted to wear pants or overalls—anything but a dress or a skirt. Mama was so disappointed that she didn't like her pretty Easter dress, but she soon got used to Charisse's choices. I remember one year Charisse asked for Lincoln Logs for Christmas instead of the doll my parents wanted to give her. From that point on, Charisse got things like G.I. Joes for presents. I started getting used to her being at my house, and for the most part I was okay with her until she started wanting to go places with me! My mother always seemed to want me to take Charisse with me, and I hated it! I was only around twelve years old, but I knew having my little sister trailing behind me would take away some of my cool points.

Beverly, Charisse, and I had to share a room, which was very small, and each of us had a twin-size bed and a small dresser. It was very crowded, and Charisse being messy did not help. She had to make a trail through her clothes to get to her bed. The room was a disgusting pink color that reminded me of some medicine that my mother made us take when we had a stomachache. Each of us kids had chores to do. My sister Beverly helped my mother with the cooking, and I got the awesome task of doing the dishes most of the time. I have been struggling to remember what Charisse's chores were, but I have come to the conclusion that she didn't do anything but irritate me, which she did extremely well!

Charisse and I always seemed to get into fights when we were growing up. I was very thin, and Charisse was always on the heavy side. Looking back, I guess we were jealous of each other for very different crazy reasons. Charisse was jealous of my size, and I, of her color. It's amazing the prejudice that African American people had toward each other. I would like to say that we have outgrown the pettiness that is associated with the color of our skin, but I still see it from time to time. Anyway, Charisse and I would get into fights like siblings do, but it always seemed to end up with me on the floor and Charisse sitting on top of me bouncing up and down. Most times I was able to get to the phone that Mama kept up in little spot in the chimney wall. I would pull it down with the hopes of hitting Charisse on the head as it fell. Sometimes it worked and knocked her off of me; however, when it didn't hit her, I generally was able to get the phone and dial my father's number to call for help. Charisse was usually smart enough to get off of me before my dad arrived, and when she didn't, Daddy would spank her butt.

Speaking of spankings, that was something that I got in abundance from my mother but rarely from my father. I remember one time we all got dressed up to go for a ride in my father's new car. I think we ended up going to Freeport, Illinois, which was about twenty-five miles from Rockford. It was one of our favorite places because of the Dog n Suds restaurant. I remember us all squashed in the backseat talking about what we wanted to order when we got there. Now, my father was as meticulous about his car as he was about his clothes. My father used to press his boxers, and all of his suits were tailor-made. So we should have known better than to expect to eat in Daddy's car! We were very disappointed until one of us kids passed out some bubble gum, and we all began to chew, and some of us were even able to pop gum or blow bubbles. We didn't think our parents were paying attention until I saw Daddy looking in his rear-view mirror and saw the scowl on his face. He yelled at us to get rid of that gum before we got it on his leather seats, and we immediately threw it out of the window and felt like that would be the last time we heard about gum. Wrong, when we got home about an hour later, what did we see? Every piece of our bubble gum was stuck to the side of Daddy's new car! He was so mad at us he told us to get in the house and prepare for our spankings. We all lined up from the oldest Beverly, to the youngest Charisse. Daddy went down the line spanking Beverly and then Melvin, but when he got to me, I looked up at him with tears in my eyes, and he told my mother he couldn't do it. He handed the switch to my mother to hit me and Charisse. My mother promptly handed it back to him and told him to complete the spankings. I heard someone softly crying, and I knew it was none of us kids, so I looked at my father and saw tears running down his face as he spanked me. That was the first and last time my daddy spanked me; it was obvious that neither of us could go through that trauma again.

Four

We were given an allowance once a week, but I decided that it wasn't nearly enough to take care of my candy habit! So, I opened up my own business. I began to make mud pies, only I called them brownies. I sold plain brownies for three cents, and brownies with nuts (small rocks), for five cents. I would get up early in the morning to make the brownies, and when the sun came up, they were ready to bake! In the afternoon I would load my wagon and start visiting my customers. My best customer was my next-door neighbor Mr. Saulter. He had a standing order for a dozen brownies with nuts; that was sixty cents' worth of penny candy a day! Let me just say my dentist loved to see me coming, because the money Dr. Ritter made off my mouth was criminal!

I decided that I was too old to be selling brownies made from mud, so at the ripe old age of twelve, I started looking for another business venture. I was finally able to find a job babysitting for the Horton family. They lived around the corner from our house, so I was able to ride my bike. Let me stop for a minute and tell you how I got my bike. I had asked for a bike for my birthday and was told that maybe I would get one for Christmas later that year. Well, remember I grew up in Rockford, Illinois. Now, where was I going to ride a bike on December 25 in Rockford? It didn't make sense to me one little bit, so I decided to figure out a way to get my bike sooner. I was having a hard time coming up with a way to get my bike, but my dad helped me without knowing it. About a week after my birthday, my father arrived home from work driving a brand-new 1964 Pontiac! Now, I was only twelve years old, but I knew that a car cost more than a bike, right? So where was my bike? I have always been a daddy's girl, so I walked up to my father and asked where my bike was. He looked at me with a sly grin on his face and said that the new car was my birthday present! At first, I got upset, but after thinking about it, I decided to take him up on his offer, only I didn't intend to let him know what I had in mind just yet!

Daddy went to take a shower (I guess he had plans to take "my birthday" gift out for a spin)! While he was in the bathroom, I located his keys and went out to the car. I adjusted the seat up as far as I could, but my feet barely reached the pedals. I had seen my parents drive many times, and I thought, how hard could it be? I was able to put the car in reverse, and I started backing out of the driveway! I remembered my parents always looked in the mirror hanging from the front window when they backed up, but I couldn't see in the mirror! The car started moving, so I tried to stop it, but my foot kept slipping off the brake pedal, so I put my foot on the other pedal, which happened to be the gas!

Well, by the time I got to the middle of the street, my dad was running out of the house screaming at me. I thought I should be the first person to try out my birthday gift, so I did! Now I had never heard my father curse before, but he was saying some words that I (to this day) have never heard! He jumped in the car and knocked me to the passenger's side where I immediately started with the waterworks. I think it finally dawned on me that I had messed up! My father drove back into the driveway and carried me inside. I offered to walk (after all, I was twelve years old and practically a teenager), but I don't think he heard me.

After my parents calmed down, they finally checked to see if I was all right! While they were checking me over for injuries, I tried to come up with an excuse for my actions. My father asked me why I took the keys to the car and tried to drive it. This was my "make it or break it" opportunity, so I looked up at my father with tears in my eyes and reminded him that he said the car was my birthday gift, and since I know that parents never lie, I thought it was! What could he say, nothing! He gave me a hug and said, "Daddy is sorry. I should have never told you that it was your gift. That was my mistake!" Now I almost fainted when he said that. I had never heard either of my parents admit to making a mistake! I felt I had accomplished a huge milestone for all kids! My father told me to go and wash my face, that he had some place he wanted to take me. We went to Kmart, and I got my bike!

My mother hated when my dad would give in to me, and she made no secret about her feelings. Mama said that ever since I was burned with the coffee, Daddy had treated me special. I guess you're wondering about the coffee. I was around four or five, but I will never forget it. My father was eating breakfast, and Mama had just poured him a cup of coffee, and my father had this habit of pouring some coffee into the saucer so it would cool off faster. Now, unbeknown to me, he had just poured the coffee when I wandered into the kitchen. I wanted Daddy to pick me up and put me on the stool next to him, so I reached up and touched the countertop to get his attention. Well, I got his and half of Rockford's attention when I screamed as coffee started traveling down my left arm! After getting me to the emergency room, my parents found out that I sustained second-degree burns. My father always blamed himself for that incident and the permanent scar that it left on my arm. I know now that I was pretty gifted in the art of using guilt to get my way.

Five

I started working for the Hortons as soon as school was out. As I mentioned earlier, they had five children: four girls and one son. Their oldest daughter was not much younger than me, but I was known in the community as a very responsible and trustworthy young lady! My days became pretty routine after the first week. I had to be at the Hortons' Monday through Friday mornings at or before 7:00 a.m. I was in charge of getting everyone up and making sure they washed up and dressed before coming downstairs for breakfast. I generally gave the kids cereal, toast, and juice for breakfast; sandwiches, soup, and fruit for lunch; and an afternoon snack. Thank goodness, I didn't have to be a Hazel the maid and clean the house. The kids were very good about doing their chores, and Mrs. Horton kept the house in good shape for having five kids! I got paid every week. Now, I don't remember how much money I made a week, but let me just say, I was bringing home more money than Beverly and Melvin did from their summer jobs! I thought I was going to be in control of my money, but Marion Hall informed me that the majority of my hard-earned money was going toward my school clothes and supplies in the fall, but I didn't mind as long as I eventually got to spend my money. I loved working with the Hortons' kids. I played games and went to the park with them so they could swing and slide. We listened to music and danced! I am so glad that none of the kids got sick during my watch. I don't know what I would have done if they had.

Before I went away to college, I had several more babysitting jobs. Coincidently most of them involved me going steady with a boy who lived near the house I worked at. I guess I was just lucky that way! I remember one particular Friday after I got paid, my mother allowed me to go shopping for a new outfit for my girlfriend's first boy-girl party! I got the cutest outfit I could find at Rockford Dry Goods, even though we "Negros" had to use the back door. When I got in line, I noticed my money was as green as the white girl in front of me! I was so excited about this party; everyone but everyone was going to be there. I had practiced in front of the mirror until I had my moves down pat! I even knew how to slow dance because Beverly's boyfriends taught me while they waited for Beverly to get ready for their date. My girlfriends and I had plans to pass out our phone numbers to some of the cute guys who were supposed to be there. I even talked my mom into pressing my tangled hard to comb hair! Around 6:00 p.m. I started getting my clothes ready for Saturday evening. I had already endured sitting between my mama's legs and getting my hair done. I had even taken my bath!

This was going to be the party of the summer, and I was going to be one of the best-looking girls there and probably the best dressed. I had just started getting dressed when I heard my mom hanging up the phone.

I thought, *Good, now she won't make me late!*

However, instead of getting ready to take me to the party, my mother called me into her bedroom. I thought she wanted to see how nice I looked in my new outfit or maybe take a picture with Daddy's new camera. But no, to my dismay, my mother calmly informed me that I wasn't going to the party! I looked at my mother and wondered if she had lost her mind! There could be no other reason for her to be saying those words to me. She had promised I could buy a new outfit, she had promised that I could go to my friend's party, she even promised she would drop me off and pick me up when the party was over or when my curfew ended, whichever came first.

Now she was sitting in her red velvet chair in the corner of her bedroom telling me I couldn't go! I tried to calm myself down because even though she had promised me all those things, she was still my mother, and I had to speak to her with respect, or she'd be sending me outside to cut a switch. So I asked God to give me the words to say because He knew I couldn't come up with anything that wouldn't get me killed! Finally I calmed down enough to ask her—why, why was she trying to ruin my life? I knew she could tell how upset I was, but she didn't appear to care!

She told me in a very calm voice, "I have a bad feeling about this party."

She could have said, "I heard that a storm was heading this way." Or maybe that she wasn't feeling well, so I had to find another ride or even that I had to put some gas in the car so she could take me. But no, she "had a bad feeling about the party"! What was I supposed to do with "a bad feeling"? I turned around and stormed out of her room and went to my room to prepare to die! I felt like dying because I couldn't go to the party my friends, and I had been talking about it all summer! All of my friends expected me to be there. More important, I expected myself to be there! I cried all night long, while my mother kept coming to my bedroom asking if I wanted to go to get ice cream! Really, ice cream! I wouldn't even talk to her. I just kept crying until I fell asleep.

When I woke up the next day my eyes were red and puffy, and I was still upset about missing the party of the summer! One of my mother's friends called her and told her to turn on the news; they were talking about a shooting that had taken place on the south side of town. Mama turned the radio on the local station, and we all listened to the reporter talk about a teenager being shot at a party on Island Avenue last night. It never dawned on me that he could be talking about the party that I was supposed to attend. But as fate would have it, it was the same party, and the girl who was killed was standing right next to the friend who had invited me to the party! I realized that I probably would have been the one shot had I gone! That was the last time I questioned one of my mother's "bad feelings." It also is the story that I told my kids when I got "a bad feeling" about them going somewhere!

Six

My childhood might have appeared normal, but it was just the opposite! Why, because my mother, Marion Louise Shannon Hall, was a special education teacher at the same school I attended! Out of all the schools in Rockford, Illinois, why did she have to teach at my school? My older brother and sister had moved on to the junior high school before Mama came, but I wasn't so fortunate. At first my mom assured me that I wouldn't even know she was there. Well, I found out that she was there real quick when I was caught talking in study hall. I was trying to explain something to my girlfriend Vickie when Mr. Kufalk noticed my lips moving! Now Mr. Kufalk (the principal) was ordinarily very nice, but on this particular day he crossed the line and became my enemy. He picked up the microphone (that could be heard all over the building) and said as loud as he could, "Lauretta Louise Hall, please stop talking." He did not have to play me like that; he could have simply come over to my table and ask me to stop talking, but no, he had to put my business all over the school! I sat there hoping that for some reason my mother had stepped out of the building and missed the announcement, or she was having trouble with her hearing that particular day and didn't happen to hear!

Well, I wasn't blessed to have any of the above situations to happen, so who came running out of her classroom but my mother! Study hall was about over, and it was time to go to math class with my favorite teacher, Mrs. Covert. I loved Mrs. Covert; she was the coolest teacher at William Dennis, and my older brother and sister had been in her class when they were at Dennis, and we all agreed she was the best! Well, anyway, I thought I would just hide in the bathroom in between classes and run to the math room right before the bell rang. It sounded like a good plan at the time. I ran into the bathroom and hid in the last stall and left the door cracked so I could hear the warning bell and make my escape! Well, the warning bell rang, and I sprinted out of the stall thinking I had gotten one over on my mother! Just as I was about to reach the bathroom door, it opened, and I'm sure you can guess who stood on the other side—my mother!

I had never seen my mother so mad before. She grabbed me with one hand and started swinging her belt with the other one. She tore my butt up while I tried my best not to scream so my friends couldn't hear me! It felt like she spanked me for an hour, but it turned out to be just a few minutes. When she finally stopped, I thought maybe she would let me lay down in the nurse's office because there was no way I was going to be sitting down any time soon! Well, I was wrong again. My mother grabbed me by my arm and dragged my behind to Mrs. Covert's room. When I got there, I asked the teacher if I could just stand in the back of the room until class was over, but before she could respond, my mother excused herself and informed Mrs. Covert that Lauretta Louise will be sitting down in her regular seat, and that was that!

My friends were jealous of my apparent status, having a mother who had a college education and taught special education and a father who was known as one of the best body-and-fender man in Rockford, Illinois. My mother was a very unique woman, especially for the neighborhood we lived in. We lived on the west end of town. In fact, we actually didn't live in Rockford; we lived in Winnebago County. For a while we did not even have running water or sewer; instead, we had a well and a septic tank. I remember how thrilled we were when the city extended their sewer lines in our direction. It's interesting the things that make you smile when you're young; it took so little back then. We were also the first in our neighborhood to get a colored TV. I can remember the whole family gathering in the living room in front of this huge cabinet with a record player at one end and a small, small screened TV at the other end. It was so small we used to take turns sitting in the middle (the coveted spot with the best view).

My mother and father were so proud of our home. I remember them entertaining club members at cocktail parties; my mother would shine up her brass and glass serving cart and her crystal ice bucket. We would clean for days. Everything had to be just so for their guest. The worst job was cleaning the center of attention, our one and only crystal chandelier. I hated that light. It had teardrop crystals that each had to be cleaned individually with ammonia or vinegar and water. My mother was also a collector of everything! I guess a lot of the things that she collected were valuable if only to her. I just remember each piece of brass or glass had to be cleaned and polished to perfection. The cocktail parties weren't all bad, we had some of the best food that we sampled as we were putting out the trays of food, and we fought over the leftovers when the guest were too drunk to care any more about the food.

When I think back to my childhood and what was special to me, I remember I used to love watching Westerns with my daddy. My favorite character was Bat Masterson. He was a good-looking white man, and he sure knew how to dress. I convinced my daddy to buy me an outfit just like Mr. Masterson's, and I took a picture on a pony that a man brought by our house once a week. I wish I knew where that picture was. My husband (a true Western fan) would love to see me all made up, and my grandchildren would get a kick out of seeing Grandma dressed as a cowboy!

Seven

My favorite thing was attending Providence Baptist Church in Rockford, Illinois. I joined church and was baptized when I was five years old. I was so small that pastor held me in his arms like a baby! When questioned by my pastor Reverend Vaughn why I wanted to become a member of the church, I stood right in front of the congregation and told them about my personal relationship with God and how Jesus was His son. I went on to tell them that Jesus bled, hung, and died for my sins. Pastor Vaughn said that I knew more than some adults.

I was also a majorette in our Angelic Choir and band. We used to march in parades with our white tasseled boots and batons. I also loved singing in the Angelic Choir standing next to my best friend Diane. My mother was the director and musician (this was not a benefit)! My mother seemed to be harder on her own children (as not to show any bias) than any other kids. She also had three other women working with her. One was Diane's mother, Mrs. Ceola Pearson, so Diane and I couldn't get away with anything!

My mom did not like our neighborhood, she was okay with working there—and even living there—but she did not want her children to associate with any children who lived on the west end.

Oh, there were a few exceptions, maybe three or four, and my circle of close friends were not always in the group of the exceptions. At first, my mother tolerated my outside friends, but eventually she told me to stop associating with anyone who hadn't made the cut! I didn't always do what my mother wanted me to do. I thought she was being very unreasonable, and I stated as much on more than one occasion. I tried to convince her that my "going with" a member of the worst-known family on the west end; the Summer's family was a good thing. I was thirteen years old and thought I *loved* Porter! My best argument was reminding my mother that the reason we had not had our house broken into like everyone else in the neighborhood was because I was Porter's girl. My mom did not agree that this justified me "going with" Porter, so I had to sneak. I memorized the shape of my mother's car headlights and was able to spot them as she turned the corner of Pierpont and Preston. I knew that after that turn I had a couple of minutes of kissing left before she made it to our house. Let me tell you, Porter was worth every scary moment I spent defying my mother!

Thank goodness, my father was very different from my mother. I think it was the difference in their upbringing. Not only did he know a lot of people in our neighborhood, but my father's business was also located on the west end of town, and so were a lot of his customers. My daddy was definitely my hero, and when I was around twelve, I realized that my parents were more different than I thought. I knew that they had arguments sometimes, but don't most parents argue? I also knew my daddy sometimes went out with other women (sometimes they were in the car when he came home to change). Oh, he always tried to tell us kids that she was one of his customers, and he was just giving her a ride home. I didn't believe that, but I figured that he had other female friends because he and my mom didn't like the same things—i.e., going out to the local clubs or private basement parties. I could justify just about anything my daddy did because he was my hero.

My father used to frequent a dinner/dancing club called the Eldorado, which was owned and operated by the Hawks family. My father and mother were both friends with most of the Hawks family. In fact, some of them went to Miles Memorial CME, my mother's church. Eldorado, the best club in Rockford, not only had the best steaks in town, but upstairs over the restaurant there was also a bar and a dance floor. Of course, I was too young back then to go upstairs, but my father used to take me to the restaurant for dinner on special occasions. On one occasion my father took me out for my eighteenth birthday, and that night he got special permission to take me upstairs for one dance. I was so excited, I could barely climb the stairs, and once I was upstairs, I didn't want to come down. When I turned twenty-one, I started going to the Eldorado as often as I could, and I hated it when they closed the club.

Eight

My youngest brother, Dennis, was born June 10, 1964, and he made quite an appearance. Dennis weighed ten pounds and six ounces. I remember I wanted to use some of my allowance to buy the baby something. Mama suggested I buy him some socks. I went to the dry goods store that was attached to "the big store" and brought some newborn socks. They were white with a black-and-red stripe at the top. I was so proud of my gift I took them to the hospital for the baby to wear on his first ride home. When we arrived to pick up Mama and Dennis, the first thing I did was open the receiving blanket and look at his feet. I immediately started crying because Dennis didn't have the socks on! Mama tried to calm me down in between my tears, and I finally listened when she said the baby's feet were too large for the socks! Dennis was the prettiest baby I had ever seen. He was not only large, but he also had the most beautiful skin and big, soft curls on his head. He had a way of looking at you that just made you melt like butter. No one could resist him. I remember thinking, *Now our family is complete with five children and two parents.* Or so I thought!

One day when I was looking after my little brother Dennis, our parents called us into the living room for the dreaded "we're getting divorced" talk. The first thing I thought about was my mother's special friend, Mr. Koss, and how he had been around a lot lately! I didn't like Mr. Koss for a lot of reasons. The main reason was the "meetings" that my mother made my sister Charisse and I attend. Charisse and I used to have to sit in the car at the park while Mama would visit Mr. Koss in his car. To this day we don't know why our being there was necessary, and we will never look back on those meetings as a beautiful memory. Our parents tried to explain all the reasons that this decision would be good for the whole family, but I didn't believe a word of it! I totally blamed my mother and Mr. Koss for my daddy leaving me! My whole world fell apart right in front of my face. Mama tried to say that things weren't going to change that much. The only difference was that Daddy wasn't going to be living there anymore. I knew that Daddy went out a lot and sometimes slept over to one of his friend's houses. I was devastated and started acting out.

It was around that time when I started running away from home. At first, my mother freaked out; after all, we did live on the west end of town! Mama finally realized after the second or third time my "running away" was only a bus trip to my father's apartment! Around the fourth visit, I met Lamont, he lived upstairs in my father's apartment building, and he was fine! Lamont had the most gorgeous eyes I had ever seen, and boy, could he kiss! My father was a lot easier going about me having a boyfriend at thirteen, so I had a wonderful time for about a year, and I realized that divorce wasn't so bad after all!

When I was around fourteen my whole world fell apart again when the house that I had spent my entire life in caught fire. My younger sister Charisse woke us up after all, because of Charisse's junking part of the room, she was the only one able to get to the door in a hurry using the path she had made. Beverly and I rushed out of the room and found my little brother Dennis standing in the dining room where the fire began. I'm not saying Dennis started the fire, but I often wondered why he was just standing there! Thank goodness, the fire inspector said the fire started in the corner of the dining room because of bad wiring. I guess that lets Dennis off the hook. I remember being terrified and trying to put the fire out with dirty dishwater from the sink, and of course, this made the fire worse. When we decided it was a useless, we grabbed Dennis and ran. My sisters, Dennis, and I were the only ones home at the time. My mother and older brother, Melvin, were gone. I can't tell you how I felt watching all of my things burning in the house I had just slept in. Part of me wanted to go back in and save some pictures, clothes, or my huge collection of 45s and albums. But I felt the heat from the fire and reconsidered my desire to run back into the flames. The neighbors started coming out of their homes and trying to help save some of our clothes and other valuables. Our neighbor Mr. Salter put some of our things in part of his garage. Fires are devastating enough by itself, so we were just happy to have everyone out and accounted for.

The fire took place on December 31 (New Year's Eve) in 1965. I was to turn fourteen the following April. Well, that year my mother brought all of us girls granny gowns alike. Picture this, bright orange-and-white granny gowns with caps! That was probably my most embarrassing moment, having our neighbors (and some of the cutest firemen I had ever seen) see me in that granny gown. Later I reminded myself that at least we were alive. Our house was so damaged that we had to move out until it was rebuilt. We moved into a motel near our house, and we got two rooms. The boys got one room, and my sisters, Mama, and I had to share the other one—yippy! I always wanted to sleep over in a motel, but this was not what I had imagined. Sharing a bed with my sister was definitely not my idea of a wonderful vacation.

The day following the fire was a Sunday, and Mama said we didn't have to go to church and that God would understand us not going. I was outraged, I reminded my mother that it was because of God that we were saved from the fire, and we needed to go to the church and thank Him! My older brother, Melvin, and my sisters gave me the evil eye because they didn't want to go. But I put up such a fuss, my mother made my sister Beverly take me to church, (suddenly being the only one besides Mama with a license wasn't so great)! All the way to church Beverly complained that we smelled like smoke because we were wearing outfits that were salvaged from the fire. I ignored her and kept thanking God that we were alive. I knew that it was only by His grace and mercy that we made it out of that house!

Nine

As you might have noticed, I was one of those rare kids who loved going to church, and I went as often as I could. I attended BTU, Sunday school, served on the junior usher board, and when I reached thirteen, I joined the Imperial Choir! I loved singing in the Imperial Choir. My best friend Diane and I couldn't wait to get into the young adult choir. It seemed like thirteen would never come. We used to march in from the back of the church to songs like "We've Come This Far by Faith." I felt so important as I walked down the aisle with my friends. Our parents and other members of the congregation watched as we marched (they wanted to make sure none of us had gum or talked in the sanctuary).

One of my fondest memories was living in the church parsonage. Our pastor, Reverend George Hines, was kind enough to let my family and I live in the parsonage while our house was being repaired. Rev. Hines's wife and children were not scheduled to join him until their school let out in June, so he volunteered to stay somewhere else so we could move out of the motel. I loved the parsonage mainly because it had an upstairs. I envied any of my friends that had upstairs bedrooms. I thought that was so cool! The fact that the house was on the south side of town was definitely a plus for my mother. Staying at the parsonage had its good and bad points. We were much closer to the church, so I could walk there by myself, but we were also living just down the street from my grandparents. Now I was crazy about my papaw (my father's dad), but I wasn't very close to my grandmother (Mama Mae). I didn't think she liked us kids too much because she gave us rotten Christmas and birthday gifts. Maybe I should explain. My uncle Clarence had a lot more kids than my dad had, and I guess that's why she gave my cousins dolls and trucks and why she gave us mittens and socks!

It probably would have been better if my cousins had gotten their gifts at a different time than we did! But as family often does, we were usually together at Christmastime at our grandparents' home. It was kind of fun, because it was not often that we were able to see our cousins on my father's side. Much later I would find out that my grandmother had a lot of respect for me, and because of her opinion of me, I met and married my Oliver!

It took over four months to put our house back together. We also had to get new appliances and have our furniture cleaned and our three Dunkin Phyfe tables leather refinished. We didn't have many clothes left from the fire, but a lot of people donated to us, so we were okay. We were able to move back home right before my fourteenth birthday. I was sad about no longer being close to the church (and my new boyfriend across the street from the parsonage), but I was glad to get back to the west end!

We always attended vacation Bible school, which usually lasted a week. The summer after the fire, our pastor asked for volunteers to teach one of the vacation Bible school classes, and no one raised their hand. I was asked to teach a class, and I was surprised and honored to be asked and gladly accepted. I thought this would be great practice since I wanted to be a teacher when I grew up. I found out that I would be teaching a group of boys who were eight years old. I was not much older than my students, but I was more mature in so many areas. I had the best time teaching the class; the boys were great and did not give me any trouble. I had to prepare lessons ahead of time because the boys kept me on my toes with questions. To my surprise, most of the class accepted Christ at the end our weeklong session. Also much later I was blessed to run into a few of my students when they became adults, and two of them had become pastors of their own church! All I could say was praise the Lord!

Diane and I had been friends since we were toddlers, and I thought we would be best friends forever until I met Bettye. Bettye was one of our pastor's daughters, and as I said earlier her family moved to Rockford when their school year ended in Mississippi. Bettye was very different from Diane and I. She was very straight laced and very much her father's daughter. Bettye was a year older than Diane and I, and she had a sister one year younger than us named Gwen. We all started hanging out together along with a few of my cousins. We all sung in the Imperial Choir and went to BTU class together. Bettye's mother (our church's first lady), Mrs. Blanch Hines, was our teacher.

Mother Hines (as I eventually called her) was very strict, but we all loved her because she was such a good teacher, and we learned so much from her. She made us want to study harder because she was so pleased when we knew the answer to her questions. Mother Hines was someone whom I grew to respect more than most adults I knew. I admired her strength and sweet disposition and the fact that she did not take any mess off any of us! Mother Hines mostly taught us girls how to respect ourselves and not let boys take advantage of us. And even though I never went without having a boyfriend, I also never gave it up until after I graduated from high school unlike so many of my acquaintances. When my mother died from cancer in June 1992, Mother Hines told me that she was my mother now. When Oliver and I became engaged, I asked Mother Hines to help me to be a good minister's wife for my husband, Oliver. Mother Hines stressed the importance of being a partner in my husband's ministry and not to ever take away from his ministry and position in the church. I learned that I shouldn't draw attention to myself in a manner that is disrespectful. I was instructed to dress in a respectful manner, in clothes that Christian women should wear. Some of the things Mother Hines taught me were just confirmations of things I had learned from my mother.

Because of our strong involvement at church some of the teens got a chance to go to Milwaukee, Wisconsin, for a Baptist Sunday school conference. Bettye, Diane, and I were among the girls chosen to go. We were so excited to be chosen and looked forward to going to Milwaukee. There was only one problem: My grandmother Mama Mae was our chaperon. We were scheduled to stay at a woman's house who attended the hosting church in Milwaukee. She was very nice, and she and my grandmother were around the same age and hit it off immediately. We had a variety of classes during the day and had service in the evening most nights. Well, the conference was almost over, and the adults decided that we could have a free afternoon to do something different before going home. Diane and I and most of the other girls started to make plans with some of the teenage boys we had met at the conference. We all decided to go to the movies that afternoon. I knew how my grandmother was, so I decided to make it almost impossible for her to say no to our little outing. We also had to convince Bettye to go, so I searched the paper for something acceptable to both of them. It just so happened that the movie *The Bible* was playing at a theater near the church. I told the boys about the theater, so they knew which one to ask permission to go to. I thought we were all set when my grandmother agreed to let us go, and we found out that the boys' chaperon had also agreed until I told Bettye what our plans were. She refused to go saying that we should not be meeting boys at the theater. It was against the rules. Really?

I thought about just leaving Bettye with my grandmother and the host lady until I remembered that she knew all of our plans and would probably tell the adults. We finally convinced her to go along with us by telling her we wouldn't sit with the boys, that we would just go and enjoy the movie. Well, we lied to her. We had all picked out the boy we would sit with, and Bettye would just have to go along with our plan. She ended up sitting next to me and my "date" and pouted the whole time we were there! Thank goodness, when we returned from the movies she didn't rat us out to Mama Mae or to her parents when we returned to Rockford. Bettye fussed at me for what seemed like forever after that incident, and I swore I would never put her in that position again. Bettye and I remained friends but didn't hang out as much after that. Now that we are older and our husbands are friends, Bettye talks to our husbands about how "wild" I was back in the day. Bettye and I ended up going to different high schools and kind of grew apart socially. But Bettye and I still hung out at church especially when her older brother Sam's brother-in-law, Leslie, came to spend the summer with Sam and his wife, Gwen. Leslie was tall, dark, and good-looking! All of the girls wanted to get his attention, but he chose me because I ignored him. Eventually, I enjoyed spending time with Leslie, mostly we hung out with a group of teens from our church, but everyone knew we were an item.

One Sunday afternoon our church went to Beloit, Wisconsin, for afternoon service. The Imperial Choir had to sing, so we all jumped into whatever adult's car that was going. It just so happened that Leslie and I ended up riding in the same car. What a coincidence! After our choir finished singing, I decided to go downstairs to use the bathroom and get some water before the preaching started. I had just finished in the bathroom and was getting ready to go back upstairs when I noticed Leslie standing by the water fountain motioning for me to join him. When I reached him, he told me he had a special song he wanted to sing to me! I had never had anybody sing to me let alone sing me a special song, I thought I had died and gone to heaven. I didn't know that Leslie could even sing until he looked at me and sung "The Bells" by the Originals. I had never heard the song before, but I will never forget the first few words: "I'll never hear the bells if you leave me." I was in love!

Leslie had to go back to St. Louis when school started. We kept in touch for a short time, but long distance relationships are hard to make work.

Ten

I have always been blessed or cursed (depending on what is going on that particular day) with ample breast. I used to get teased by both boys and girls in middle school, but in high school things changed. I will give you an example: I used to sneak and wear my sister Beverly's sweaters to school. I figured she wouldn't know since we didn't see each other that much. But what I didn't count on was the difference in our chest size and that my breast would make a larger impression in her tops; that would be the cursed part! The stares I received from the boys in high school were definitely the blessed part! I don't remember a time in my high school career that I did not have a boyfriend or two. Yes, I was a bit fast back then! I really thought I was special because most dark-skinned girls like me didn't get much attention.

My first year in high school was also the first time I went out with a Caucasian boy. His last name started with a *G* and mine an *H*, so he sat directly in front of me. He was so cute and had the most beautiful blue-gray eyes I had ever seen. Tom did not dress like the other boys in my class. Instead of wearing blue jeans, he wore dress slacks and shirts. He reminded me of a nice-dressing Fonzie on *Happy Days* only better looking. He was Irish, and because my mother's maiden name was Shannon, I thought I was Irish too (little did I know that the name Shannon was given to my ancestors by their slave masters). One day Tom talked me into skipping a class and going over to one of his friend's house for an impromptu party. I decided to go, but I was a little nervous about the outing. I had met Tom's brother who was a junior at Auburn High, but I had never hung out with any of his friends. I didn't know what kind of things Tom liked to do; all we had done was talk on the phone, and he walked me to class whenever time allowed. The house we went to was about a mile from school, and I paid attention to the landmarks as we passed them so I would be able to get myself back to school if I needed to. We listened to music and danced—let me take that back, his friends danced. I didn't like the music they were playing and had no desire to dance to it. Tom kept asking me if I was okay, and I lied and said yes, but I knew that if he really knew me, he would know I was extremely uncomfortable. I thought we were about to leave and go back to school when the guys decided to smoke before we left. I may had have been fast, but smoking was not something I did when I was fourteen. I started coughing and gagging until Tom asked his friend to take me back to school, that I didn't sound so good. Needless to say, my relationship with Tom did not last long, especially after my father found out. Daddy was pretty cool with me liking boys as long as they were the right color and coming from Mississippi. White wasn't one of the colors he approved of.

    Riding the city bus to school was so much fun because we had to go downtown to change buses to get home. We used to tease the Muldoon Catholic girls when they got on the bus wearing their uniforms. Later I became good friends with a couple of Muldoon girls, and they reminded me of how terrible my friends and I were to them. When I look back at that time in my life I realized I was jealous of those uniforms. It meant that their families had money enough to send their kids to private school. When you're fourteen you start looking at the differences between your family and someone else's family. I realized that just because my friends from the west end thought we were rich didn't mean that we were. We weren't the poorest family, but there were a lot of things we didn't have. I realized that if my sister Beverly hadn't been able to sew, I wouldn't have had the neat clothes my friends envied. We were poor, but we knew how to look rich!

Eleven

The sixties were a difficult time for African Americans even in the North. Prejudice was everywhere in America. I remember having to use the back door to go into the local Woolworth and Rockford Dry Goods stores. I also remember having to sit in the balcony at the Coronado Theater. We tried to make the best of a difficult situation by making the white kids think that we were having much more fun than they were by sitting upstairs. I also realized during that time that even though there was prejudice in the North, it was much worse in the South. After all, we didn't have bathrooms and water fountains marked for colored or white only!

On one of my trips to the South I almost found out what the hanging noose was all about! My cousin Judy, her mom, and I were on our way to a carnival where we would be working at a stand selling sandwiches and pop. We decided to stop at a fruit stand, and my aunt told Judy and I to go get a drink and use the bathroom before we got back in the car so she wouldn't have to stop again. Well, when I looked at the Colored Only sign over the water fountain and saw how dirty it was, I decided I would just get some water from the clean fountain that happened to have a White Only sign above it. I was just about to wet my whistle when this hand circled around my neck and grabbed me back. I was about to go off when I realized it was my aunt. She asked me if I wanted to get all of us killed and pointed to the sign and asked me to read it out loud to her. I learned a very valuable lesson that day, drinking from a dirty water fountain was the only way to stay alive in the South!

In 1968 when I was about to turn sixteen, I decided to test for my driver's license. I had studied so hard for the written test during driver's education I felt pretty confident about that part of the test. However, I had very little experience behind the wheel of a real car (we had simulators in class). Having an older brother and sister with a license, my mother didn't see much need in me getting one, and my behind-the-wheel inexperience showed that! Finally the big day arrived: April 23, 1968, my sixteenth birthday. I wanted to take the test that day so the date issued on my driver's license would coordinate with my birthday. My family tried to talk me out of going that day; they thought I should wait a couple months seeing as though there was no hurry for me to drive. Looking back, I realize they didn't think I would pass and get my license! Well, I surprised everyone (including myself) and passed with flying colors. Because my mother didn't think that I would pass, she agreed to my request to drive for my birthday. So my mother let me drive in downtown Rockford by myself that afternoon, and I was so proud and wanted everyone to see me. I was warned not to pick anyone else up because they could be a distraction, so of course I immediately went over to my favorite cousin Corlet's house to pick her up (like a lot of teens, I usually did the opposite of what my mother told me)!

I decided to drive down West State Street, the main street in Rockford, so everyone could see us! However, there was just one little problem, I was looking back at them! I had just smiled and waved at a rather nice-looking guy, and when I turned back, the light had changed, and everyone had stopped except me! I rear-ended the car in front of me, and the wonderful experience ended. The police arrived (they didn't have far to go). I was in front of the Winnebago County Courthouse and got my first ticket! I thought my tears and sad look would get me off, but it didn't help. I got yelled at by the driver of the other car, the policeman, and my cousin! Needless to say, I wasn't allowed to drive much after that!

However, my sixteenth birthday wasn't all bad. My parents gave me a fabulous sweet-sixteen birthday party at Booker Washington Center. At the time the center was under the direction of Deacon Davis, a past member of the Harlem Globetrotters. Deacon Davis was awesome, and he and my parents were friends, so they got a good deal on the rental of the gym. It was to be the party of the year, and I invited everyone I knew from school and church. I wanted all of my friends to finally meet, and of course, I wanted lots and lots of gifts! Perhaps I should mention that I had a party every year for my birthday. I don't remember my siblings having any parties. I guess they didn't want one. I invited almost fifty kids, and almost everyone I invited showed up. However, there was one problem: My mother insisted on being there! And Marion Louise Shannon Hall wanted every light in the building on (I felt like I was at a basketball game instead of a party). I forgot to discuss the dos and don'ts of a teen party with my mother, not that I think she would have done things differently. I thought I would die of embarrassment when the kids started asking me why all of the lights were on. I told them the truth—that my mother thought everyone would get busy (fornicate) if any of the lights were turned off! It was bad enough that my friends were complaining, but something I feared happened. Kids were starting to leave and take my gifts with them! I wanted to crawl under the bleachers and die! I just knew that I would get the reputation of being the girl with the terrible party! Just when I thought I couldn't take any more humiliation, my father and his cousin Jr. came back from a store run with food and cans of pop, and my party was saved! The two of them promised my mother that if she agreed to dim the lights, they would chaperone and make sure no one made any babies! My party and my reputation were saved, and I got to keep all of my gifts (after all, isn't that the main reason for having a party)?

The summer after my sixteenth birthday I met Raymond! We met at Washington Park Recreational Center, which was a couple of blocks from my house and his. How can I describe Raymond? He was around six foot two inches tall, and he resembled the actor who played the lead in the movie *Amistad*, Djimon Hounsou, only he looked better. Raymond was my first real bad-guy boyfriend. I used to mess around with Porter, but I was a kid and didn't know about relationships, but what I had with Raymond was serious! Raymond had been in a juvenile facility, so Mama was very much against my seeing him. Mama just didn't understand Raymond; he was so deep! He used to write me letters that made me cry; they were so romantic. I immediately felt like we would be together forever. I was in *love*. With my mom feeling the way she did about Raymond, we had to see each other away from my house, so we spent a lot of time at his aunt's place in the projects. His aunt Jessie was so sweet, and she and I got along right from the start. She was impressed with the fact that my mother was a teacher even though at the time she was working at Amerock Company instead of teaching. She was definitely impressed with my family, and I really liked her because she was so accepting of my relationship with her nephew; in fact, she thought I was good for Raymond.

Raymond and I saw each other as much as we could, but because both of us were working part-time jobs, our times together were few and far between. Raymond got into trouble during one of those times we weren't together, and I didn't find out until a week after he was gone to a juvenile detention center. Raymond's aunt said he wanted to write to me, but my mother had to give her permission because I was under eighteen years old. At first my mother said no until I kept crying and begging her, and she decided to let us correspond. I think it dawned on her that him being in jail meant I couldn't see him. Raymond and I wrote back and forth for about six months until I got tired of not having someone to go out with and broke things off.

I dated different guys in high school and a few I met at church or when I was hanging out on the south side at Diane's house. Sometimes we walked down to Lathrop Elementary School where a lot of kids hung out. Mostly I just had a good time attending every party I was allowed to go and learning all of the newest dances. I had also spent a lot of time at my cousin's house. My Aunt Carrie V was the best, she smoked cigarettes, and my cousin Corlet and I would take turns lighting her cigarettes on the stove. We usually took a detour after lighting the cigarette so we could get a couple of drags before we gave it to her. My mother and Aunt Carrie V were very close, and it always puzzled me because they were so opposite.

My mother was very strict and wanted to know where we were at all times, while my aunt was cool about letting us just hang out. Sometimes my cousin's friends would stay there all night without getting permission. If someone called and asked if their child was there, she would reply, "Honey I don't know. They could be." Then she would yell upstairs and check. I loved spending the night over Corlet's house; there was always a lot of people and excitement there.

I also enjoyed my other cousins. I even played football with some of my cousins and their friends. My mom didn't have a problem with me playing football until one Saturday when we were in the middle of a game, and I got tackled when I didn't even have the ball! Needless to say, that was my last time playing football with boys.

I also liked hanging out with my girl Harriett. We sometimes double-dated, but mostly we went driving. We drove around for what seemed like hours just listening to music and sometimes parking. I remember one of my favorite songs was popular, and we listened to it over and over again—"Love on a Two-Way Street" by group called the Moments! My boyfriend's nickname was Mookie. Neat name, right! Anyway we lost track of time, and before I knew it, my curfew had passed! No one else in the car had a curfew, so I didn't want to mention mine. I noticed that we were over by my aunt's house when I realized I had to use the bathroom, so I asked Mookie to stop and let me run in for a moment. Well, when I knocked on the door, it was around one o'clock in the morning, but of course someone was up. There was always someone up at my aunt's house! Anyway when I got inside, my aunt asked me if I knew just how much trouble I was in. I tried to play it off and said, "Know how much trouble am I in?"

That was the only time I saw my Aunt Carrie V upset with me. She told me to shut up and listen, which I did! She informed me that my mother had called numerous times looking for me and had even contacted the police and the fire department trying to find me. I thought why the fire department, but I knew better than to ask. I just promised her I would go straight home. Well, I went straight home as I promised, but I wished I hadn't.

I had just walked in the door when my mother grabbed my neck and threw me in the house. I was trying to say good-bye to Mookie, and she completely ignored him and slammed the door in his face. I tried to tell her that I wasn't through saying good night yet when she backhanded me across the living room! She asked me just what did I think I was doing strolling into the house at two in the morning. I reminded her that I was going to be eighteen years old in a couple of weeks! She informed me that there was no guarantee that I would make it to eighteen! After a few minutes when I thought she had calmed down, I took a chance and looked out the front window to see if Mookie had left yet. He hadn't, so I told my mother that Mookie was waiting to get permission to take me to church later that day so could I go back outside to let him know it was okay. I figured Mama would be happy to know that my boyfriend wanted to come to church with me, but I was wrong! My mother opened the door and told Mookie to forget my phone number, forget where I lived, and especially to forget me! Then she said, "Now get the hell out of my driveway and never come back again!"

Well, needless to say, that was the last time I saw Mookie until I was a grown woman with four kids!

Twelve

I was dating a guy named DeWayne during the last part of my senior year, so I assumed I would be going to the prom with him, but I was wrong. You see, DeWayne was antiestablishment and didn't believe in attending things connected with school such as proms! I couldn't believe I didn't have a date for the prom. Oh, I could have gone with someone else, but all of the cute guys already had dates. I told DeWayne how disappointed I was with his decision, and he informed me that he already had a date set up for me with his friend Quincy. Now I knew Quincy, and he was cute even though he was a year younger than me, so I agreed to let him take me. My sister designed and made my dress. It was sleeveless and pink, and Beverly made me a stole to go over my shoulders. It was the most beautiful dress I had ever seen!

Quincy and I went to the prom with my girlfriend Harriett and her date, Michael. My mom and dad insisted on taking pictures before we left for dinner. After they ran out of film, they finally let us go. We had decided to go to the Pink Pony, so Quincy and Michael had made reservations for us earlier that week. The food was wonderful. When we got to the prom, all of my friends talked about how pretty and different my dress was. I told everyone that my sister

Beverly had designed and made the dress. Quincy was able to drive his parents' white duce and a quarter! We were the envy of everyone who saw us! Quincy and I never had thoughts of being together past the prom, but that one night was magical! We danced away the evening at the prom and went to the postprom party. I am glad that I didn't go with my boyfriend because as the post prom started to end, most of the couples decided to go to the motel to officially end the prom. Quincy, Michael, Harriett, and I rode around for a while and went home with my virginity safely intact.

Shortly after the prom and before graduation I met Donnie! The Imperial Choir that I sung in had our annual day in May, and we invited youth choirs from other churches to be our guest. All of the choirs were scheduled to march in together, so we all assembled in the basement of the church. My girlfriends and I were checking out the boys in the visiting choir, and my eyes rested on Donnie. Our eyes met, and we both kind of stared at each other. Diane asked me who I was looking at, and when I motioned toward Donnie he smiled at me. Diane agreed that he was cute, and then it was time for us to march upstairs. After the program I wondered if I would ever see him again, and as I prepared to go home, there he was. Donnie asked me if he could call me sometime after we exchanged names. I gave him my number and told him a good time to call me, and we left it at that. The next day he called, and we talked for what seemed like hours! I found out the next day that because he lived out of town but still in Illinois my number was a toll call for him but not for me. I thought that our friendship was doomed because there was no way Marion Louise Hall was going to allow her daughter to call a boy!

Donnie had gotten in trouble with his parents for staying on the phone so long and running up their phone bill, so I told him I would ask my mother if it was okay for me to call him. I was totally surprised when Mama agreed. Looking back I think she was so glad that I had met someone other than DeWayne that she agreed. Donnie had been real sick when he was child and missed a lot of school, so he was a year behind me. That didn't bother me at first because he was one of the nicest people I had ever met, and he was so respectful toward me. Donnie and I both had part-time jobs that summer; he worked at a local grocery store, and I babysat for a really nice couple a few miles from my house.

I loved babysitting for the Smiths. They had a little girl around three and a baby boy that was about seven months old. Donnie and I didn't have much time to date, so I decided to ask the Smiths if he could come over sometimes while I was babysitting. I assured them that I would not let his visits interfere with my job, and they agreed to try it and see how it worked. Donnie came over two to three times a week. The kids loved having Donnie around, and since he had a car we were able to take the kids to the park sometimes with their parents' permission. Sometimes I went to church with Donnie, his parents, and his two sisters. I loved spending time at their house. They were very nice people and welcomed me with open arms.

I especially liked when Donnie would come to Rockford and attend church with my family. I could tell Mama liked him because she would let him stay around past my curfew! My summer was wonderful, and I hated when the end came, and it was time for me to go away to college at NIU. I tried to console myself with the fact that NIU was just in DeKalb, Illinois, and only about forty-five miles from Rockford and a little over an hour from Donnie. What I hadn't counted on was that Donnie was still in high school, and I was thrown into a completely different world full of people from Chicago and Indiana. Donnie and I tried to keep in touch, but with phone calls being tolls each way, we ended up writing a lot of letters. Donnie was able to meet me in Rockford when I came home, which wasn't often. You see, being in college and away from home meant freedom! Freedom that I wasn't used to and honestly did not know how to handle.

Thirteen

What can I say about NIU. Our university was situated in the middle of cornfields and barbed wire, which were the two main things that DeKalb was famous for. I was assigned to Grant North my first year on campus. Because my ACT score wasn't the best, I entered NIU through the CHANCE Program. That was cool because most of the kids I met my first week were also part of the CHANCE Program. And added bonus was that my brother Melvin worked at the CHANCE office while he was attending graduate school. My mother decided that I should major in elementary education (I wanted to be an attorney). You see, my mother never had the opportunity to finish college and get her four-year degree, so she decided that one of her children would get their BS in education, and I was the most likely candidate. Oh, I loved working with children and had been babysitting since I was twelve, so I could understand Mama's reasoning. However, I was beginning to have an interest in the law after watching countless *Perry Mason* episodes. I thought he was cool, and I was impressed with him winning most of his cases. I especially liked when he would discover who had committed the crime and tricked them into confessing during the trial.

I discovered a very important place my first week on campus: the student union. I was informed that frat parties were held there every weekend. During these parties the frats and sororities stepped or performed before the crowd. My brother was an Omega, and I had visited him at U of I a couple of times when I was in high school, and I had seen some step shows, and I loved them. I remember one time the Omegas had told everyone on campus that one of the frat brothers had passed away suddenly. The Omegas decided that they would still step because their brother would have wanted them to carry on. When they walked in the union ballroom, they carried a casket that was supposed to represent their fallen brother. They put the casket on one side of the room and slowly started to step; they all appeared to be really sad about their brother's death, but they started their performance. All of a sudden the supposedly dead brother threw open the casket and sat up, people started screaming, and some women even fainted. He jumped out of the casket and got in line and started stepping as if he had been there all the time. The Omegas won the contest that year hands down. Nobody even wanted to step after the Omegas finished. I saw lots of step shows and even performed in a couple, but I never saw a better show than the one I saw at U of I. Unfortunately (for my grade point), I went to every party I heard about, including the after parties that took place in the Barn, a snack shop that was downstairs and connected Grant North and Grant South. My first semester I didn't do much homework. You see, the professors did not take attendance, and they didn't call your parents if you didn't attend class. So as you might have guessed, my grades suffered to the point that I was put on academic probation by the university and put on notice by my brother and parents. Melvin was so embarrassed by my poor grades he threatened to disown me as his sister! I tried to explain myself, but everyone, including me, knew it was going to parties that messed me up. Needless to say, I got my act together the next semester and dramatically pulled up my grade-point average. I knew that I had to figure out a way to keep my grades up and be able to party with my friends. I think that is when I became obsessed with organizing everything in my life from my sock drawer to my college education.

BACK TO THE BEGINNING

My first year at NIU I was assigned a random roommate. Lisa was from a rich (mostly white) suburb near Chicago named Elmhurst, Illinois. Lisa was okay with me as long as she stayed on her side of our tiny room. Well, one day Lisa ventured over to my side and asked if she could touch my skin. Needless to say, I wasn't sure how to take her and asked her what her problem was. She turned completely red and said that she had never seen a *Negro* up close and wondered if my skin felt anything like hers. I let her touch my hand and told her I hope all of her questions were answered because she would never be allowed to touch me again. I realized then and there that Lisa wasn't comfortable being around African Americans, so I had my friends come over a lot and stay a long time. Every time Lisa came in the room, it was full of African Americans, or Negros as she called us. I could tell she was very uncomfortable, and by the end of the first semester, Lisa moved out! Having always shared a room with someone, I found that I really enjoyed living by myself, and because Lisa had moved out so abruptly, the university didn't have time to replace her, so I had the room to myself the rest of that year. I enjoyed living by myself so much I decided not to have a roommate during my sophomore year. It was during my sophomore year that I met the man who would eventually be my first husband.

My next-door neighbor Katie was a very jealous-hearted girl and seemed to want everything that everyone else had. I was dating a guy named Tim at the time. Tim was a very nice-looking, quiet young man who had lived in Rockford when he was a child. Tim and I studied together, walked to the show near campus, and hung out at the Barn most evenings. Katie had seen us together on many occasions, and I noticed she did not appear to be happy about our relationship. A rumor started circulating around our floor that Katie wanted my man. I guess I did not realize just how much she wanted Tim until the day I met Butch. One night I was in my room studying when I heard a knock at my door. I assumed it was one of my girls from the dorm and opened the door without looking through the peephole. Now as you may have guessed, I didn't look in the mirror, comb my hair, or straighten up my room before opening the door, and there he stood.

Alton (Butch's his real name) was around six foot tall, thin, and at the time very nice looking. He asked for Katie, saying he was a good friend of hers and had dropped by to see her. I informed him that Katie lived next door and pointed him in the right direction and closed the door. There was another knock at the door a couple of minutes later, and upon opening the door Butch was standing there smiling at me. He explained that Katie wasn't home and asked if he could have some paper to write her a note. I invited him in and gave him what he needed and tried to look busy while he wrote his note. When he was through, he handed me his information—i.e., name, phone number, and address—instead of a note for Katie. It wasn't until years later that I found out that Katie had sent Butch over to try and get me away from Tim so she could get with him herself. Butch said he thought I was attractive and asked to take me out. Before I could respond, he asked me to think about it and call him tomorrow with my answer. Later that same evening I called Tim and told him that I wanted to start seeing someone else and broke things off with him. I called Butch the next day and accepted his invitation, and so it began!

Fourteen

My first clue should have been his nickname Bud Man and the Budweiser emblem on his jacket. The fact that he worked at a liquor store near campus should have been the icing on the cake. Butch had more charisma than most, and he knew how to use it. He reminded me of the Pied Piper the way he attracted people to himself. All he had to do was mention that he might go to a party, and the crowd would just show up. Butch was three years older than me and lots of years ahead of me when it came to being worldly. He introduced me to his friends from Chicago, and my popularity grew overnight. I was known as "Butch's girl" by everyone on and off campus. Butch also had a beautiful voice and used to serenade me from below my dorm window. I was the envy of all of my friends and even some of my enemies. Sometimes he even had flowers delivered to my dorm room. I was only twenty years old at the time, and like most young ladies my age I had never had that kind of attention before. My girlfriends used to tell me that Butch had "blown my nose open wide enough for a truck to go through." As Butch's lady one of my new "duties" was to be a hostess, so I spent most of my spare time at Butch's apartment entertaining him and his friends.

Most of Butch's friends were in school or had finished school. After a while it became very apparent that my boyfriend was the only uneducated one in the group. I found myself rationalizing Butch's lack of education by saying to myself that he has street learning, and that makes up for his lack of book learning. I was impressed with Butch's dancing skills; he could do any dance that came out. I never had to worry about lack of attention at a party because when I wasn't dancing with Butch, I was dancing with one of his friends. Butch could also bowl and had been on some bowling teams. One time we went bowling with some of our friends, and Butch decided to liven things up a little by doing one of his many tricks. I had never seen this particular trick, so I was as interested as everyone else in the group. Butch announced that he was going to bring the ball behind him and then throw it between his legs and make a strike.

I thought to myself, *He is going to look like a fool when he misses.*

But I soon saw that I and several others had underestimated my boyfriend; he not only made the strike, but he also did it several more times to prove that it wasn't just luck. My whole world began to change slowly but steadily. I promised myself that I would not be persuaded by the fast life and liquor, but it happened. You can't be with a crowd and not be influenced by what they do. I continued going to classes and working part-time as I had before I met Butch. But my friends saw me differently; they acted as if I were married to Butch already. I stopped getting asked to dorm parties because even though I had a room in the dorm, I was rarely there. As I mentioned earlier, some of my friends envied me, but some of them were really concerned about the steps I was taking with Butch. Because I was so in love, I explained their concerns away without really considering the points that they were trying to make. I wanted so badly to make my relationship work with Butch. I had already invested so much of myself in loving Butch that I already felt I had gone too far to give up now. I had allowed Butch to take me to "another level" since we had been together; in other words, he had gone where no man had gone before!

When I look at some of the young ladies today and how early in their life they go all the way with more than one young man, it saddens me. When I was a teen, we were reminded time and time again that our bodies were very precious and should only be given to the man whom we marry. And when I was a teen, I was so scared to move to that level with one guy, especially after my mother told me how much it would hurt. It's amazing how much you change after that first time; that's why it is so important that you share yourself with the right person, preferably with your husband. The experience is something that you will always remember—whether it's good or bad. It will also form a bond between the two of you that will be hard to dismiss. The bond is generally only felt by the girl. Boys usually think of the girl as another feather in their hat when they succeed in going all the way. That is all you mean to them.

I was so happy. I was doing well in school and enjoying being off campus at Butch's apartment. I would cook these romantic dinners with candles and fresh flowers on the table. I hadn't done much cooking when I was growing up, but I was a fast learner, and soon I was able to fix a variety of things, and I loved keeping the apartment clean. Butch was working at the Store, a liquor store that most people went to because it was so close to campus. We did all of our grocery shopping together, and sometimes he even helped me study for a test. I spent so much time with Butch that I started losing myself in him. I didn't know it at the time; otherwise, I would have started to back away. It is amazing how much spending time with someone who has a strong personality and a controlling mind makes you so vulnerable. Butch was so smooth I didn't even notice when he started ordering my food. I probably thought that it was sweet and the way a husband would do things. Another example: I remember one day we went out shopping for clothes, and before I realized it, he had picked out my whole outfit! He told me what looked good on me and what didn't; he became my mirror. Butch also decided where we went as far as parties, or "sets" as we called them. I let it go because he did know where the action was, but as I look back, I don't remember him even asking me what I wanted to do.

For my twenty-first birthday, my mother agreed to give me a big party back in Rockford, so I invited all of my friends, and my man furnished the liquor. It was a wonderful party, and a lot of my friends came up from NIU. I will never forget that birthday for a couple of reasons: (1) It rained so hard that our street flooded, and no one was able to leave and go back to DeKalb. My mother put all of the ladies in one part of the house and the guys in another part, and she sat up all night in my grandmother's rocking chair to make sure that no one "got together" that night. And (2) Butch proposed to me that night, and of course I said *yes!*

That was April 23, 1973, and my friend Jackie and I spent the summer getting my wedding together. I insisted on getting married in Rockford at my old church with my pastor officiating. I decided to ask my girlfriend Angel to sing my favorite song; "The First Time Ever I Saw Your Face" by Roberta Flack. I didn't have the money to buy a dress, so my sister-in-law Lynn offered me her wedding dress. Butch wore a rented tux, and my friend Jackie and her husband stood with us. The church was decorated beautifully; my mother really outdid herself. We had a small reception at the community building in the Terrace Apartment complex. We had a beautiful cake, lots of fried chicken, potato salad, green beans, and rolls. When we got married on September 8 of that year, I was three months pregnant with our first son, Alton III.

During the summer before we were married my father came down to DeKalb to visit me, and he indicated to me that he wanted to talk to Butch alone so I went to the Store. While I was gone, my father offered my future husband money not to marry me (I did not find this out until after we had gotten married). My father obviously knew something that I should have known. Everything went well the first two months. Butch got a job at Rockford Products; my sister Beverly's husband helped him get a job there. Rockford Products covered my delivery and hospital stay even though I was pregnant when Butch started working there. Butch was making good money, and we were able to find an apartment on the street that I grew up on, across from my mother's house.

My first experience with the real Butch came in November, two months after our wedding. My best friend Mary came up from NIU to Rockford for the weekend, and we decided to throw an impromptu party to introduce her to some single guys. I asked Butch to keep it simple because of my pregnancy and our limited finances, but he had other plans. The party started out nice enough with our closest friends in attendance, and everyone appeared to be enjoying themselves. However, after dancing too much I started cramping, so I decided to lie down for a while. When I went back to the party, I noticed my husband with my so-called friend Amy, and they were making out on our couch! I thought I must be dreaming because he wouldn't do this in our home! Little did I know that was only the beginning! I grabbed the first thing I saw (a bowling trophy) and threw it barely missing Amy's head. I asked Butch just what he was doing, and I told Amy to get her bald head out of my house before I killed her! You would think that Butch would have been embarrassed at being caught, but he gave me a "just deal with it" look. My girlfriend Mary started screaming as she removed her earrings preparing to fight for my honor. I told everyone the party was over and to get the hell out of my house, and I proceeded to open the front door. I wanted to confront Butch then and there. Almost everyone was gone when my husband came back into the living room with his coat on informing me that he had to take that Amy home in my car! By this time I was standing in the middle of the floor screaming and crying and wondering just what the hell I had gotten myself into! After Butch left with Amy, I started crying harder and shouting louder!

My husband's cousin Marcelle was trying to calm me down while reminding me I was pregnant; he kept saying how sorry he was that Butch was treating me so badly and what could he do for me to help me calm down. I told him the only thing he could do for me was to give me the keys to his car. I was on a mission! As you might have noticed, I didn't use any curse words in this book; however, when this situation took place, I was not as close to God, so my words were very colorful, but at this stage of my life, I am not comfortable with those words any more. I don't remember grabbing a knife, driving to Amy's house, or the fact that Mary was in the car with me. I just remember arriving at her apartment building! Amy and I grew up together, and she was one year behind me in school. I had heard that Amy had gone after other women's men in the past, but I thought we were at least acquaintances if not friends. What was more disturbing was the fact that Amy was best friends with one of my girlfriends, Angel, the same Angel who had sung at our wedding just two months before. Anyway the first thing I noticed was my car (a gift from my father) sitting in front of Amy's apartment building.

By this time Mary had started to calm down, but I was just getting started. She tried to get me to just take my car and leave. But I had to see it for myself. I had to see him in her apartment! I started climbing the outside stairs to Amy's apartment almost slipping on the snow-packed steps, with Mary right behind me still pleading with me to just leave. When I reached the landing I didn't even ring the bell. I just started kicking the door, demanding to come in. After it seemed like hours, Amy finally opened the door. I pushed past Amy (knocking her against the wall) and started yelling for my husband. Amy had the nerve to say he wasn't there and told us to leave. She obviously didn't realize that she was speaking to a woman with a knife, possessed, out of control, and on a mission!

I started walking up to closed doors and kicking them in looking for Butch! Finally, he came out of what looked like her bedroom, wearing the robe that I had brought him for his birthday in June! I wondered what happened to the robe. I thought I had left it at the Laundromat! Immediately I could tell that Butch was mad at me instead of being concerned about being busted! He informed me that I had no right to be there chasing him down like he was a child! I just stood there, it felt like cement had been put in my shoes, and I couldn't move. I tried to move my feet, but I couldn't. I just stood there looking at the man whom I had exchanged vows with just two months before and the father of my unborn child.

Mary kept saying, "Girl, let's just go. He ain't worth it!"

With Mary's assistance I was finally able to move my feet and leave. We made our way back down the snow-packed stairs, and I drove my car home with Mary trailing me in Marcell's car.

Mary knew that when Butch came, home he and I had some things to work out, so she went, called a friend, and her friend drove her back to DeKalb. I had just showered and started getting ready for bed when I heard the front door open. I had assumed that Butch would spend the night at his "lady's" apartment, so I was surprised to see him standing in the doorway of our bedroom. He didn't have to say anything; the look on his face said it all. He had the nerve to still be mad at me!

Fifteen

At first he was real quiet and just stared at me. After about ten minutes Butch started going off on me, saying, "How dare you come looking for me, embarrassing me like that."

I reminded him that I had every right to look for him, and how dare he be at Amy's house! Before I knew what was happening, his right fist met my left eye. I had never been hit so hard in my life and never by a man before! I had heard about women being hit by their husband or boyfriend, but I never thought I would have to experience anything like that in my lifetime. You never know what may happen to you during your life, so you should always expect the unexpected. Hopefully what happened to me won't happen to you, but never say never because you don't know what you would do until you are actually going through it.

The blow was so forceful that I fell back on the bed. I was lying there holding my eye when he grabbed my hair and pulled me to my feet. He proceeded to throw me against the wall, and I fell to the floor, praying that he would stop hurting me! Where was the man I fell in love with, the one who used to serenade me and send me flowers? I could think of nothing to do but call on the name of Jesus! I began to pray out loud asking God to save me, to stop my husband from killing me. Suddenly he stopped. He left the room cursing as he walked away. I thought, *Finally he is going to leave me alone.*

I picked myself up just as he walked back into the room, he then grabbed my left arm, and began to drag me out of the room. Our kitchen was in the basement, and I begged him to let me go so I could get some ice for my eye.

He said, "I'll get you some ice." And he threw me down the stairs!

By instinct, I grabbed my stomach and rolled myself into a ball to protect my baby. I think I must have had an out-of-body experience because I could see myself lying on the floor, and I was standing there looking and wondering what the hell was he going to do to me next.

By the time I reached the bottom of the steps, I was hurting pretty bad, and pain was shooting through my stomach. I just knew something had happened to my baby. I just lay there afraid to move, afraid that my baby was dead. I kept thinking that if my baby was dead, I wanted to die too. I started telling God, *If You were going to take my baby, please take me too.*

Finally Butch came down the stairs and helped me up, half-carrying and half-dragging me up the stairs. By the time I reached the top of the stairs, I found out what Butch had in mind for me next. Butch decided that I needed to go home (to my mom's house) and be reraised before I returned as his wife, so he informed me that I was leaving. As I mentioned earlier our apartment was across the street from my mother's house, and that was precisely where he took me. I must interject that it was the middle of November in Illinois, and the temperature was at zero or below. I had on panties, a bra, my robe, socks, and slippers. Butch allowed me to grab my sweater before dragging me across the street to my mother's. I kept trying to go back to the apartment. I begged him to let me go or at least let me get a coat. Butch acted as if he was possessed because he paid no attention to what I was saying. He just kept telling me that I needed to grow up, and he didn't have time to raise me!

By the time we got to my mother's porch, I was so *cold* the tears had started freezing on my face. Butch left me standing there shaking as I knocked on my mother's door. After a few minutes I remembered that my mother had gone out for the evening, so no one was home. I looked across the street to the apartment and back at my mother's house trying to figure out what to do. My mother's neighbors Mr. and Mrs. Saulter must have heard crying and knocking because I looked up, and Mr. Saulter was standing in his driveway calling my name.

He said, "LaLa [my nickname], girl, what the hell is going on?"

Seeing him just made me cry harder. I was so ashamed, cold, and scared all at the same time. He came around the shrubs that separated their property and grabbed me. He kept saying, "Come on, you're coming home with me."

At that point I was so tired, I didn't argue. Plus I was weak and cold, and his warm house sounded like heaven at that point.

Mr. and Mrs. Saulter had been neighbors to my parents all of my life. Everyone used to think that he was mean because he was always yelling at the neighborhood kids for taking a shortcut through his garden. But I loved the Saulters. They were very sweet to me, especially Mr. Saulter. As I mentioned earlier he was my best mud brownie customer. Mr. and Mrs. Saulter wrapped me in a blanket and gave me hot chocolate to drink. They waited for me to start talking. I couldn't imagine what they must have been thinking. I was pregnant, bruised, cold, crying, and standing on my mother's porch looking like a homeless person. When I was able to calm myself, I told the Saulters some of what had happened and asked if I could use their phone to call my mother. I remembered that my mom was at our friend's home at a dinner party. I hated to bother her; she got out so seldom, but I couldn't continue to stay where I was, so I placed the call.

When the phone was answered, I couldn't talk. I froze. My mouth started moving, but no sound came out. Mr. Saulter took the phone and asked for my mother after he explained who he was. When Mama came to the phone Mr. Saulter handed me the phone, and I started crying uncontrollably. I couldn't talk. All I could do was cry until finally I got myself together and tried to talk to my mother.

I explained some of what happened to my mother, and at first she didn't say anything. I think she was in shock. My mother probably never expected to receive a call from one of her children crying and telling her that they had been hit by their husband of two months. After it seemed like forever, I heard her asking her friend's for their gun.

I started screaming, "No, Mama, no, please just come home. Please just come home." Our friends got on the phone and told me that they would be bringing Mama home and for me not to worry. They wouldn't give her a gun.

Sixteen

When my mother arrived home it was hard to calm her down—especially when she saw me standing before her in my robe and panties and still clutching the Saulters' blanket. The look that she gave me is difficult to describe. It was a combination of anger, pity, and disgust. Mama had warned me about Butch so many times, and being the hardheaded child that I was, I didn't listen. My mother finally calmed down and made up the guest room for me to get some sleep. I tossed and turned the rest of the night and into the morning. I woke up with very conflicting thoughts running through my head. I wondered if God wanted me to just leave Butch and raise my child alone, or if He wanted me to try to work it out and save my marriage. With my parents being divorced, I know how much my mother had to struggle to raise us by herself. I wondered if I could do this on my own. I got up, showered, brushed my teeth, and got dressed in some of my old clothes that I had left at my mom's when I got married. After eating breakfast my mother went to church. I was too embarrassed to show my bruised body.

I realized that I couldn't stay with my mother indefinitely (we probably would have hurt each other), so I tried to think about where I could go, who I could stay with. I thought about my mama Mae (paternal grandmother), but the thought of the mothballs that she strategically placed everywhere in her home ended that idea. My father lived in an apartment building for the elderly or handicapped, so that wouldn't work. My mother suggested one of her friends, Mrs. Williams and her family. My first thought was I don't think so; it would be just like living with my mother. But I started thinking about the fantastic food she always brought to church for the monthly pot-lucks and decided to go for it. Mr. and Mrs. Williams agreed having me as a visitor for a *brief* amount of time. I stayed a total of three days with the Williams and then returned home to Mama's house.

When I got home, my husband was sitting out front in our car waiting for me. I tried my best to ignore him, but when a six-foot-three-inch tall man is crying and begging for you to forgive him, it was not a situation that I was used to. My mother was calling me from her front porch, and my husband was begging me to go home with him. I began walking toward my mother's home, but I kept hearing him yell, "Lauretta please come home. I won't hit you no more." I took comfort in knowing that the faster I walked the easier it would be to tune him out. I stayed about a week and a half with my mother and then prepared to look elsewhere.

One day while sitting in my mom's swivel chair, I was confronted by my mother's roomer Paul. He came over and sat next to me. At first he just sat there and stared at me then he asked me to marry him. Besides the fact that Paul was several years my senior, he was also not my type. Still I found myself thinking about his proposal until it dawned on me that Paul was living with my mother, with no mention of moving out soon. Did he think we were going to marry and share his bedroom with the twin beds in it?

Well, as you might have guessed, I went back to my husband. He even kept his word for a few weeks, and I was able to start my student teaching in a kindergarten classroom in Barbour Elementary School. When I was younger I used to dream about going to Barbour, a lot of kids from our church went there, and most of them were popular. I suppose I thought popularity came with the school. Anyway, I had a very good experience at Barbour, the teacher I student taught with was down-to-earth and found my pregnancy to be a wonderful way of teaching the kids where babies came from. Butch was amazing during that time. He went out and purchased several new maternity outfits for me from one of the most expensive shops in town.

I knew we couldn't afford it, but I went on and on about how pretty they were and how much I appreciated them. For Valentine's Day, he brought me a special outfit and took me to see Lou Rawls at Mr. Kelly's in Chicago, Illinois. I will never forget that night, I met Lou Rawls, and he dedicated a song to me and my unborn child.

Seventeen

I delivered our first. child on March 21, 1974, at Rockford Memorial Hospital after several hours of excruciating pain. The only redeeming things about the whole experience (besides my son) were the several scratches and scars I left on Butch's arms and hands. I felt so optimistic about my life and my new child. I just imagined the wonderful life the three of us would have. Alton was the perfect baby, he loved entertaining himself, he would lie in his crib day after day making noises and smiling.

When Alton was six weeks old, Butch decided that it was time to have sex again. I reminded him that I had not been to the doctor yet (my appointment was in two days) and therefore did not have a form of birth control. He continued to remind me that as his wife I had certain duties to perform for him. I had enough experience with Butch to realize that he was not going to be reasonable, and I had better do something to protect myself. I went to the drugstore and asked for the best rubbers they had. They offered me sheepskin and charged me a fortune. I kept reminding myself it was well worth anything I had to pay to keep me from getting pregnant again.

My first clue should have been when Butch went into the bathroom to put the condom on (he had never been shy before)! I remember thinking, *Lord, please just let him do his business and get up!*

When the deed was done and Butch withdrew, he said, "Oh no!" The rubber broke!

My mother had told me that it was very easy to get pregnant right after giving birth, so I just lay there and cried knowing what had probably happened. Three weeks later, my doctor confirmed my suspension and informed me that I was indeed pregnant. I kept telling the doctor and myself that it was a mistake. We had no intention of getting pregnant again so soon. But neither one of us believed that it was a mistake.

When Butch came home from work I shared the devastating news with him, I don't know what I expected his reaction to be, but what I got was not one of my choices. He just sat there with a knowing smile on his face as if he had accomplished something. I reminded him that it was much too soon for me to be pregnant and that carrying a child was dangerous for both me and the child. His response was, "What's the big deal? Anyway I planned for you to get pregnant!"

As I sat there with my mouth open, he explained how he cut the tip of the rubber so I can stop wondering where that little piece of rubber went. He went on to say that I might leave him with one child, but I would never leave him with two.

Eighteen

After several attempts to leave him, I finally decided to go with him to Houston, Texas, and live with his mother. Now my only experience with his mother was on our wedding day when she burst into my dressing room at church and stated, "So you're her."

I guess that was her way of saying welcome to the family! The 1,500-mile drive to Houston was something I will always remember; the three of us (Butch, Alton, and I) made that long trip in my little red Volkswagen. The car was filled to the roof with our belongings (everything else was scheduled to come on the moving truck). Much later when Alton was a teen, he mentioned that he hated the song "Loving You" by Minnie Ripperton and really did not understand why. I explained to him that during the whole drive to Houston, that was the song his father played and sung over and over and over again.

I had a lot of concerns about moving so far away from my family and living in the midst of his. However, I was pleasantly surprised. Mrs. Shelvin was very nice to me, and whenever her son would yell at me, she would tell him to bend down (she was around four foot five to Butch's six foot three), and she would slap him.

Butch started working at an offshore oil company, his job took him away from home at times, and I appreciated the breaks. Most times Butch behaved himself at his mother's house, but he still drank to excess. One evening after Butch had been drinking all day (he was off work that week), he decided to go over to his friend's house on the other side of the Houston. Mrs. Shelvin and I both tried to get him to stay home, even though he was used to drinking and driving. That particular day he hadn't eaten anything so of course the alcohol in his system would affect him more. After he left I informed his mother that I was going to call the police and ask them to find him and stop him before he killed himself or, even worse, someone else! I gave them the license plate number and a description of our car, and they assured me they would find him. Houston is a very large city, so I gave them information regarding the area that he was driving to. It was about two hours later when we received a phone call from the Houston Police telling us that Butch had been arrested and what his bond was. I was certainly not going to pay our little money to Houston to get him out of jail, but his mother insisted and drove me to police station and gave me the money to get him out. I later found out that it may not have been the best place for a black man to be back in the '70s.

I gave birth to our second child, Edward Albert Anthony Shelvin, on February 13, 1975. I had a spinal for the first time, and I was very impressed with how pain free I felt. My doctor had to tell me when to push because I didn't feel my labor pains. I was in labor for only two and a half hours. I had the cutest student nurse with me the whole time I was in labor, and she asked if she could be in the delivery room. I was feeling no pain and told her sure. The more the merrier! Butch had to drop me off and then take Alton to his aunt's home and then come back, and since nothing is close in Houston, he didn't get back in time for the birth. The student nurse held my hand and became my labor coach. She was a very special young lady.

The day after I gave birth, the student nurse sent me a dozen red roses! While I was recuperating from labor, I had some time to think about my situation. My sons will be the same age every year for six weeks! It was like having twins but not!

Shortly after Edward was born we moved into our own apartment. I was getting a little tired of being the cook at his mother's house. I should have guessed that would happen when I saw that her kitchen looked like it had never been used, because she informed me it hadn't. But the things that happened after we moved made me wish we had stayed with Mrs. Shelvin. I really liked our new apartment; we were able to go out and buy new furniture with the money we saved from living with Mama Shelvin. I remember thinking my life was about to turn around. I thought our family was going to start resembling families I had seen on TV like *Leave It to Beaver* or *The Cosby Show*, two of my favorite shows. Well, no one could ever accuse Butch of changing; the Butch whom I fell in Love with and then learned to hate was back!

Butch decided that we would have a "sex schedule": every Sunday, Tuesdays, Thursdays, and Saturdays. On the other days he generally did not come home. More than likely he was participating in his other sex schedules. You would think I would have a problem with his extracurricular activities, but by this time in our marriage, I welcomed it. I became increasingly ill on "sex nights," and later I would refer to our love making as Celie did in *The Color Purple* by Alice Walker, when mister climbed on top of her and did his business. In between the sex nights, I got knocked around for GP (general purposes). My biggest concern was my children. Butch would often want to "punish" me in front of the boys. He felt that he needed to reraise me and finish the job my parents started, and he wanted his sons to know how to handle their women when they grew up.

Nineteen

When Edward was about six months old and Alton almost a year and a half, I decided I'd had enough and left. I went back to Rockford, Illinois. I was determined to return to school and complete the fourteen hours I had left so I could earn my BS. At the time I was getting assistance from the Department of Public Aid, so I talked to my caseworker and found out that I was eligible to get some assistance from the department to move to DeKalb, Illinois. My caseworker also transferred my case to DeKalb since that was my only form of income. I talked my girlfriend into sharing an apartment with me and the boys, and we got a three-bedroom place off campus. I felt so blessed that God had brought us to this point and provided me a way to finish college.

Now I had been friends with Vera for several years, but I had never lived with her before. Note to all single mothers thinking of living with a single young lady with no children of her own: don't! Vera had a problem with every car, block, or truck the children brought into the living room. I tried to explain that they were just babies, but she refused to see it my way. When her sorority began to pledge a line, things got better, for a while. Vera's pledges were constantly around doing jobs she made up, such as watering fake plants.

It was getting toward the middle of summer when I met Marvin from Baton Rouge, Louisiana. He was part of a team that was training for the Olympic wrestling team. He was around 6-foot-five inches tall and a beautiful chocolate-brown color. He was the sweetest man I had ever met, and I was instantly taken with him. I told him that I was separated and the mother of two boys. He fell in love with my sons. He used to carry both of them on his shoulders at the same time, and he told them that they were helping him exercise! Our relationship progressed very easily; he even brought over a friend for Vera. We really enjoyed spending time together. He was so different from Butch; he reminded me that all men weren't evil and lowdown. We had a beautiful summer until it was time for him to go to the finals in New York. We said our good-byes and promised to call and write, but I didn't put too much stock in it. I felt blessed for the time we did have together.

About two weeks later I heard a knock at the door, and there he stood. Marvin had been cut from the team and was on his way back to Baton Rouge. He said he just wanted to see me again before he went home. Well, what started out as a few-hour visit ended up being three weeks! While Marvin was there, I went to the doctor for my annual checkup, and he found lumps in each of my breast. I agreed to have a double biopsy the following week.

My mother agreed to keep the boys, so Marvin and I took them up to Rockford. Marvin took me to the hospital that next morning. I signed a paper stating the doctor could remove one or both of my breast if he needed to. I felt that if I needed to go back under for a removal of one or both of my breasts, it wouldn't happen. When I woke up all I saw were bandages across my chest, and it looked as if both my breast were gone. I started screaming, and Marvin walked into the room with my doctor and told me everything was okay. I was so thankful I started crying and thanking God. My friends had sent me a beautiful bouquet of flowers, which surprised and touch me. But all of those flowers were forgotten when I saw Marvin standing there with a single red rose.

Shortly after my surgery, Marvin had to leave. I thought I would never stop crying and missing him; he was the first man who had treated me as if I were special. We talked about staying in touch, and we did until I graduated in December 1976. Vera and I decided to part ways after the summer, and she moved out of the apartment. I did not know what I was going to do. I could not afford to pay the rent by myself. Plus Vera had helped with the kids, and now she was gone. I prayed and asked God to provide a way for me and the boys to continue to live in our home. I was led to speak to the manager and explained my situation.

He told me that if I were willing to take care of the building for him, he would forget half my rent every month. God had opened doors for me once again. I met some of the new neighbors in the building while I and the boys were cleaning, and we formed friendships. When school started, I had three different babysitters for the boys. The only thing was that one family was from Japan, one from Nigeria, and the other from Mexico. So my very impressionable son Alton began talking in three different languages and would get upset when I didn't understand him.

I did not have a car after Vera left, so getting around was a challenge. With my limited funds, I could not afford anything but a child's wagon. So I purchased a red wagon and pulled my sons all around campus, sometimes taking them to class so the other students and my teacher could observe their reaction to different stimuli. I met some of the most interesting people on the last semester at NIU. For example, my next-door neighbors, three men (I used to call all of them "Eye Candy), were always inviting the boys and I over for dinner (they really just wanted to play video games with the boys), but I reminded them we are a package deal. One thing about their apartment bothered me and fascinated my sons; they had a pariah as a pet. I was terrified especially when they would feed him whole hamburgers or steak, but the boys would jump up and down screaming with joy.

As I said I met a lot of interesting people. I was walking down the street one day pulling the boys in the wagon and heard some guys saying, "Hey, beautiful, can I have your number?" I heard more other complimentary things. Of course I had to stop and check out the men behind the words. I looked up, and the first thing that caught my eye was a guy name Eddie he was about six foot five, had gray-green eyes, and blond hair (I suppose I should mention he was

Caucasian). They were up on the third floor on their balcony, and Eddie ran down the stairs to see me before I could pass their building. He mentioned that he had seen me before and realized he had to meet me. We dated for a couple of months; he was a principal at an elementary school in Sycamore, Illinois. Eddie was one of the most generous people I had ever met. He insisted that I take his car when he wasn't using it. He gave me a set of keys and would drop the car off at my building whenever it was free. Everything was cool until we took our relationship to the next level, and I realized the myth about white guys and their equipment was true—at least in Eddie's case. I kept wondering where the rest of it was. I should have known better when we would discuss sex; he always said the size shouldn't matter! Wrong, and that was the end of my chapter with Eddie.

Twenty

I finished my last fourteen hours in December 1976. I stayed in DeKalb and babysat for extra money until May so I could walk with my class. Our graduating class was huge, so my mother and I came up with an idea so the boys could see me from the stands and I could see them. We went to a flower shop and had them dye three carnations a deep blue, and when I marched in with my college of education, I held up my flower, and the boys spotted me and held up theirs. I was so happy and thankful for God allowing me to complete my classes with a grade point average of 3.7 out of a 4.0, but what excited me more were that my sons were there along with my family (some of them doubters), saying I (a single black woman) could never finish college with two children. They obviously didn't know the God that I serve is able!

There was also another person (besides my family) at my graduation, yelling louder than most, my husband Butch. My family was so mad to see him there they were all shooting daggers at him and his friends. As you might have guessed, we got back together after he convinced me to move to Houma, Louisiana, with him. I had begun applying for teaching positions in Rockford to no avail, and I was becoming very discouraged. Butch suggested I apply to Terrebonne

Parish School system in Louisiana. I took a chance and applied and was hired right away. I was offered a position at Terrebonne Middle School as a seventh- and eighth-grade science and math teacher.

Butch was offered a job at a company that drilled for oil in the Gulf of Mexico, but he needed to get to Houma before we were ready to go, so he drove down alone, and we followed a couple of weeks later with his cousin Marcelle. Marcelle is a very caring person and very much unlike his cousin. The trip to Houma was so much fun for the boys and I; it was very relaxing without arguments, and much more room! Marcelle pointed out some of the sites as we passed through the South, and we stopped whenever the boys needed to use the bathroom and run around a little. Marcelle and I still remain close, and he continues to care about our family.

We moved in with Butch's aunt and uncle, his mother's brother Albert and his wife, Wanda. Wanda was a schoolteacher, and Albert was retired from the air force, and they had one child. I met several of Butch's family, and most of them lived in Deweyville, a small section in Houma. Houma, or should I say Deweyville, was so much fun. Since school didn't start until the middle of August, I had to find some other work for the summer.

I found out that Butch had lost his job because he had gone to work after drinking (surprise, surprise), and of course, he was fired on the spot! Thankfully, I started working in Butch's uncle's place as a barmaid. I never worked at a job like this before, but I loved it. Fortunately at that time I was very small and wore a size 3, because the uniforms Deedee wanted us to wear barely covered my butt! Deedee's place was the most popular night spot in Houma. Everybody that was anybody hung out there. The barmaids (four of us altogether) were expected to wait on tables, fix plates of barbeque pork and beef ribs and all the trimmings, and (when we had time) dance with and entertain the customers. I had always loved to dance, so that was my favorite part of my job and my husband's least favorite! You see, while dancing, I got hit on more times than Hank Aaron hit a baseball! Butch even had a problem with the male customers talking to me. He said that he didn't care if it was part of my job; I looked like I enjoyed it way too much!

I had saved up enough money to purchase another used Volkswagen, and I was so proud of that car. One weekend I took the car into the shop for an oil change and tune-up. That Monday, I received a call from the owner and was informed that my car had been in an accident. I started yelling and screaming asking him how in the hell did my car get into an accident in his shop.

He explained that the car had been up on the rack when one of the hydraulic lifts broke, and my car went down. He said that it could have been worse; the car had landed on the table instead to the floor, like that made a difference! I immediately start thinking about getting a lawyer and suing them. The owner, however, made a deal with me by offering me a cash settlement and a practically new Chrysler Cordoba. It was white with a gold leather top. I thought it was a fair compensation for the pain of not having my bug.

I thought that it looked like the tide had turned in my favor, but it was short-lived. Butch and I had one of our famous arguments about me working at Deedee's. While I was reminding this fool that without my job and tips, we would not have food to eat and a place to stay (we had finally moved into our own apartment), he had been drinking (of course) and took the keys to the car away from me and ran out the door. About a half hour later, I received a phone call from a friend of his informing me that Butch had gotten into a bad accident and totaled the car. I grabbed the kids, called a cab, and went to hospital. When I saw the fool, he was lying in bed and pretending to be more injured than he was. I asked him what happened, and he said that I upset him so much that he tried to take his own life by driving "my car" into a brick wall. I told Butch that I could have helped him kill himself without ruining the car—our only mode of transportation!

Twenty-One

I wondered how I was going to get to my new job in two weeks and who was going to watch the boys while I worked. Thank goodness, my sister Charisse wasn't working at the time, and she volunteered to come to Houma and watch the boys for me while I went to work. By this time, Butch had found another job working for an oil company, which paid very well. I knew we had enough income to put the boys in day care, but my husband informed me that the money he made was his and not to count on using it for something as silly as putting the boys in day care!

I really appreciated Charisse coming down; my family had given her the money! When she got to New Orleans she caught the Greyhound to Houma. I borrowed our aunt's car (until I could get another one) and went to pick her up. I was so glad to see her I started crying. I wiped my eyes and noticed Charisse was crying also. This surprised me, she very seldom cried, but I figured she was glad to see me also. I read her tears wrong, she grabbed my face and cried harder, and she asked me when was the last time I had looked in a mirror. I asked her what she was talking about; she couldn't respond because she was crying too hard.

Finally she stopped and told me that I looked like a living dead and I was so skinny she couldn't see my cheeks anymore; all she saw was my skin hanging on my face. I couldn't imagine what she was talking about. I said I had lost some weight since last seeing her, but Butch tells me all the time that I'm too fat! I told Charisse that I can't understand why I had lost weight when I eat all of the time. The folks in Houma believe in feeding you every time they see you, with all the red beans and rice, jambalaya, crab legs, and gumbo I should have been weighing a ton! I promised her that as soon as my insurance started at the school, I would go to the doctor.

Things went okay for a while until I got a phone call from the principal at my new school telling me that I could come in any time now and decorate my classroom. I had been so excited about having the opportunity to decorate my own classroom that not having any money to purchase anything was even more upsetting. I asked Butch for a few dollars, and he laughed at me and walked out of the room. I went to the school to see if some of the other teachers had some extra decorations they could spare. I was blessed to find some teachers who could give me a few things, so I spread them out, so it looked like more than I had put up.

I prayed that God could make up the difference so the children wouldn't notice how sparse the decorations actually were. Things went well for a few weeks, and (besides getting hit on by some of the students) it was pretty uneventful. Things were quieting down at home, and I thought maybe, everything will be all right. I suppose that's what I got for thinking. I came home one Wednesday and walked into the house thinking about the science tests I had to grade and the lesson plan I had to complete for the next week when I heard this loud crash in the kitchen. When I ran in to investigate, I saw that Butch was staggering around knocking things off the counter and table. I tried to help him stand so I could get him into the bedroom, but before I could do this, he started cursing and hitting me.

I told Butch to just go into the bedroom and sleep it off like he normally did. I reminded him that I had to finish my work for school the next day. Why did I remind him about my job? He lit into me telling me just because I taught school doesn't mean that I was smarter than him. He went on the say that he could do my job much better than me, and I had everyone fooled at the school. I tried to ignore him and get back to work when he decided to rearrange my papers by putting some of them on the floor and some on the couch. Every time I attempted to pick them up, he would hit me again. I was trying not to scream. I didn't want to alarm the boys or my sister.

But sometimes, despite our best efforts, we can't stop from screaming when someone is punching you. My sister ran into the room and introduced her left fist to Butch's jaw. He just went down like a ton of bricks. She sat down on his stomach (for an instant I laughed because she used to sit on me when we were kids to stop me from calling my father for help); anyway, she commenced to punching him in his face, neck, and chest. I can't begin to explain the feelings that I had at that time; it was a mixture of joy and sorrow. Joy because someone was doing what I wished I could do, and sorrow because I realized that "this is my life!" I called the police, and after an hour or so, they arrived.

We (my sister and I) explained what had happened and asked that they arrest Butch on assault charges. That was a waste of time. Houma, Louisiana, is a very small town and almost every black person there is somehow related. One of the policemen was Butch's fourth cousin, twice removed. He took him outside and walked him around the apartment complex (to give him time to cool off). Right! Not long after they came, they got into their car and left. Did you know that abusers don't like for the victim to call the police, and if they do, the matter becomes worst? Well, calling the police was one of the worst things I could have done.

I told my sister to take the boys to the playground and stay there until I came and got her (I did not want the boys to see their father beating me and calling me out of my name any more than they had to). After a lot of coaxing, my sister left with my sons. After that all I can remember is my sister shaking me and trying to get me to respond. She informed me that when it got dark, she brought the boys home and found me on the floor. Butch had taken the car and left. Charisse helped me get up and attempt to gather my work up. Butch had torn the children's test into pieces and thrown some of them away. I just sat there and cried. I realized then and there that I couldn't do this. He wasn't going to let me teach. I called the principal the next morning and tried to explain my circumstances and gave him my oral resignation with my apologies. A few days later I took the school's books and papers (all that weren't torn) and returned them to the school along with my written resignation effective immediately. That was my first and only attempt to work in the field that I had graduated from school with. Shortly after I stopped working, my sister told me she had to leave and return to Rockford, because she wanted to finish school.

Twenty-Two

Since we finally had medical insurance, Aunt Wanda convinced me to go to the doctor and offered to keep the children for me. My doctor weighed me and informed me that I weighed about ninety lbs. I explained that I had been eating a lot, but I would get up from the table and almost immediately have a bowel movement, so I stayed hungry. After I made arrangements for the boys, I agreed to being admitted into the hospital. The doctor did a series of tests, including the upper and lower GI. The next day the doctor came in with the results. He informed me that I had an infection in my intestine that was very much like a tapeworm. He gave me some medications and told me to take it easy for about a week. When I arrived home, I informed Butch of what the doctor said. He reminded me of all the work that I had to do, and he wouldn't be helping me with any of my duties but expected the house to be clean and food on the table when he arrived home. Maybe I should mention that my "very busy" husband was not working at the time (he had lost yet another job) and generally spent most of his time with one of his girlfriends.

Butch noticed that I was making friends with some of women in the apartment complex and became irate.

"You don't have time to hang out and talk to these women. Find something constructive to do when your work is done," he told me.

To ensure that his orders were carried out, he informed me that we were moving soon. I asked why and where we were going, and I got slapped and told that he was the only one who needed to know the details. Later that week I found out that Butch had gotten another job and had been working for about two weeks. We moved into another apartment in a much nicer neighborhood. I loved the apartment, it was new, and I think that we were only the second family to live there. We settled in very quickly, the boys found children their age, and I met what would later turn out to be my very best friend, Lettie.

Lettie and her husband lived on the same floor that we did, and she was so down-to-earth and not related to Butch! Lettie reminded me of some of my friends whom I went to NIU with. Her son was one of the children my boys played with, so we were able to spend a lot of time together. I remember that when our two families got together, we would have the best time.

I loved the new place and made the mistake of telling Butch how happy I was and thought I was pregnant. A few weeks later I found out I was pregnant with our third child, Emtesha. Butch announced that we were moving. I pleaded with him to let us stay; he insisted that we needed more room for the baby. We already had three bedrooms. How much room did we need? We ended up moving about a mile and a half from the apartment complex that we had lived in.

I'd like to describe the so-called beautiful house that my husband had picked out for his family. It was a shack on stilts. I remember it was the ugliest green color. As I mentioned before, it was up in the air because of the water. We lived next to a Louisiana swamp. There were just two bedrooms and a bathroom (that resembled an outhouse).

We had moved from a modern, well-kept apartment, with cathedral ceilings, nice neighbors, close to schools and stores, to live in a barely standing house out in the middle of nowhere! The street hadn't even been paved, and our nearest neighbor (next door) appeared to be a groupie for the KKK! I found out just how much she hated African Americans one day when the boys accidently kicked their ball over into her yard. I knocked on the door and was informed, "We don't like you people. Don't throw your toys in my yard and swing on my fence and don't knock on my door again."

Finally, her husband threw the ball back for the boys (the next day while he was out in his backyard). Being in Louisiana in the '70s, I did not expect a knock at the door announcing the delivery of our welcome basket, but I also didn't think my neighbors would be putting on white sheets like ghost or burning a cross in my yard. I reminded the boys to be very careful with their toys, and if anything went over the fence again, they might as well wave good-bye because it wasn't coming back!

For once Butch had kept a job for longer than a month, and I assumed that he was making good money. However, up to that point, I had never seen a paycheck or stub from any job Butch had ever worked on since we had been together, so the amount he made didn't matter! Around a month went by, and I was about to go stir crazy; I was not allowed to drive the car (even though sometimes, Butch's cousin would pick him up). He would leave the car under the carport and take the keys. We had a phone, but Butch locked it up in the trunk of his car while he was away! As I mentioned, we lived about a mile and a half from the main street, so the boys and I only walked to our friend's house about once a week. Lettie did not have a car, so she couldn't come and get us. Sometimes we would walk all that distance only to find out she wasn't there. So, we would rest for a while and walk back home.

Life continued to be the same until, one day, I received a registered letter from my mother saying that the family reunion was to be held in Rockford that year (our family met for a reunion every two years, so everyone tried their best to make it). My mother sent the boys and I plane tickets to come to Chicago, Illinois, on the following Wednesday. We were so excited, the boys and I started dancing around the shack until we heard some of the floor start to give in. The boys started talking about their cousins from Illinois and Memphis (all the ones they remembered) and getting more excited by the minute.

I tried to calm them down before the "warden" got home, because we still hadn't gotten permission to go. To my surprise, Butch agreed that it would be good for us go and visit with my family. I began trying to find clothes for the boys that weren't worn or patched, and I came up with just one set of play clothes for each of them. I knew that my family would not care what we were wearing; they just wanted to see us. But I just couldn't take my kids up there with no decent clothes for them to wear. I asked Butch when he got paid, and he claimed not until the Friday after that Wednesday that we were scheduled to leave. I reminded him of the small amount of clothes that the children and I had to take and asked if he could borrow some money from one of his uncles and pay them back on Friday when he got paid.

Butch was a very proud man and refused to let his family know the state that we were in. He told me to write a check at Kmart on Tuesday evening, and he would replace the money in the account on Friday (back then, stores didn't run the checks to their bank before the ink dried). I begged him to please not forget to put the money in the bank on Friday. Lettie took me and the kids to the store, and I spent a little over $300 dollars on the children and myself. As far as I could figure Butch got paid around $3,000 in each check, so there shouldn't be a problem.

The boys and I went to the reunion, planning on staying about two weeks. My mother reminded me that she would love to have us stay longer. You know sometimes God will place things in your spirit, and this was certainly one of the times. I had a very uneasy feeling about returning to Houma. I called Butch and asked him if anything had changed since we left. I explained that the boys and I could stay longer and that it would not be a problem. He said that everything was just fine and for me and the boys to come on back. I agreed, but my spirit wouldn't let me be okay with leaving. I called Butch again and asked if he was absolutely sure everything was fine; he insisted it was. I specifically asked how his job was and if there were any changes that I should know about before I returned. Butch started accusing me of having a man in Rockford, and that was why I did not want to return.

I knew how crazy he could be so I agreed to return that weekend. Butch picked us at the airport in New Orleans, the boys were glad to see their father, but that uneasy feeling had gotten stronger since we landed. We lived about fifty miles from New Orleans so I wasn't surprised when the boys went to sleep when we were about halfway there. I asked Butch what days did he work the following week (I know he usually worked straight through and then had time off). He decided to come clean and address the uneasiness that I had been dealing with for the last week. Butch informed me that he had quit his job and had gotten a better one. I began to ask questions about this new job, and I did not like the answers I received.

Butch informed me that this job paid only one time a month, and he wasn't due to get his first check for three weeks. When I asked him if he had any money left from his other job, he said that he only had $20 dollars! Then I found out that the money was to last us for the next three weeks! I prayed the rest of the way home. When we got home I went to the kitchen to see what type of food was available for me to use until Butch got paid. The only thing that was in the icebox, was a case of Budweiser beer! No bread, no meat, not even one egg. I don't know why I was surprised; this is just the type of mess Butch would do!

I asked him what we were supposed to eat until he got paid. I was informed that it was my problem, and I had better fix it. The boys were hungry and started crying when they saw that nothing was in the icebox except what their daddy called "my medicine." I gave the boys the rest of the snacks I had purchased at the airport and put them to bed. I asked just what was I supposed to feed our kids, let alone his pregnant wife. He popped the top on his beer, sat on the couch, looked at me, and smiled. I went to bed asking God to please have mercy on my kids and me.

When I got up the next morning, Butch had left for work leaving ten of the twenty dollars with instructions to purchase enough food to last until he got paid. I woke the boys up, we took showers, and we left for our one-and-a-half-mile walk to the nearest store. I went over my girlfriend's house, and, thank God, she was home. I asked to use her phone to make a long-distance call. I called my mother and father and explained my circumstance asking if there was anything they could do to help us (I was so ashamed to have to ask them for help after they had flown the boys and I to Rockford and back and took care of us while we were in Rockford). My mother started crying, and my daddy started cursing.

Twenty-Three

My parents agreed to wire me some money after I promised them I would not use any of the money to feed my no-good husband. I didn't know how I was going to accomplish their request, but I promised I would. My friend Lettie borrowed her mom's car to take me to pick up the money and to the store. I purchased enough food for the boys, and I then borrowed three ice chests from Lettie and her mother. I put the chest underneath the house on stilts and told the boys that we were playing a trick on their father, and we would let him in on the secret in a few weeks.

    I fixed food for the children and me, fed them, and put them to bed before their father came home. When he got there and asked what was for dinner, I told him that his $10 were gone and that the food he smelled came from Lettie and that she had only brought enough for the boys and I. Now of course Butch got mad. I expected as much. He threw me around and called me out my name, but I figured he would have done the same thing even if I had fed him. He took us to fast-food places on the weekend so were able to do this for a couple of weeks. His aunt brought food the last week. He finally asked his family for help; he was getting hungry! Finally the last week arrived, and I thanked God for keeping us. Butch was getting paid at the end of the week! The boys and I were breathing a little easier, and for the first time in a long time, Butch appeared to be in a good mood.

It was Tuesday afternoon, and I had put the boys down for their nap when I heard a knock at the front door. I assumed it was either Lettie or one of Butch's relatives, so I didn't even check to see who it was. I just opened the door. Standing on the porch was a policeman or state trooper. I couldn't tell which. He asked me if I was Lauretta Shelvin, and I replied that I was. My heart stopped. I just knew that he was bringing me news that someone in Illinois had died or something equally as serious. He introduced himself, showed me his badge, and asked to come in. After I offered him something to drink, he accepted and sat down in the chair I offered. The policeman assured me that no one in my family or Butch's had been injured.

I thanked God that everyone was okay, and then I learned that he had a warrant for my arrest! I couldn't think of anything I would be arrested for and asked if he was sure he didn't want Butch. He showed me the warrant, and I couldn't believe my eyes. The warrant was for writing a bad check, and I sat there scratching my head trying to remember writing any check let alone a bad one. It finally dawned on me that it must be the check I wrote before I left for the reunion in Rockford, the check my husband had promised to put money in the bank to cover. I started praying and crying. Then I explained that I was pregnant and had two small boys, and I just couldn't go to jail! He tried to console me and tell me how sorry he was to have to be the one to serve me. The patrolman asked where I was originally from because I did not sound like I was from that part of the country. I told him that I had been born and raised in Rockford and had graduated from NIU in 1976 and then came here to teach.

I was getting ready to explain my situation regarding my husband when he stopped me and told me he had also gone to NIU and had graduated in 1975. He told me he was from Rochelle, Illinois, and had moved here because his wife was from Louisiana. He asked me what kind of situation I was in and told me he would like to help if he could. I explained to him the type of person I was married to and how he had promised me that he would take care of the check. I also acknowledged that I knew it was against the law to write a check without having sufficient funds in the bank, but I didn't feel that I had a choice at the time. He told me that he could pretend that I wasn't home and return on the following week.

I thanked God and the trooper and promised him that I would do my best to take care of the matter. After meeting my sons, he left and said, "I will be praying for you and the boys."

I told him that God had to be the one to send him to my home, and I give Him all the credit for things working out the way they had. I promised him once again that I would do my best to straighten out this situation. After the trooper left, my sons and I walked up to my girlfriend's apartment to use the phone. I called Butch at his job and told him about the trooper and asked him what we were going to do. Without any hesitation, he told me that it sounded like a personal problem, and I should figure out how to handle it.

I reminded Butch that I was pregnant and that we had two young sons at home. He said that he would ask someone in his family to watch the boys if I had to go to jail. I kept yelling at him that he had promised me he would put the money in the bank. What happened? He replied, "I guess I forgot."

I just dropped to my knees and began to pray. I knew that God was the only way I could walk away from this, not have my baby in jail, and be able to take care of my sons.

While I was on my knees, my girlfriend called her mother. Later I found out her job. She clerked for a judge and said she would speak to him about my situation. After explaining in detail what I had been dealing with for the past five years, Lettie's mother called back and asked to speak to me. She explained that the judge wanted to see me as soon as possible. Lettie agreed to watch the boys, and her neighbor took me to the courthouse. The judge was very kind, but firm. He asked me if I would be able to come up with the money to cover the check and pay the fine. He explained to me that I would need around $490. I knew that Butch would never give me that kind of money, but I knew that God would make a way, so I told him I could.

The judge said that I would still have to go through the booking process and let them take my fingerprints and take mug shots, but he would arrange for me to be released in Lettie's mother's custody.

The judge told me that I had to make him another promise before he would agree to help me. At this point I would have promised almost anything! He said I had to promise him that I would leave Butch and return to Illinois. I promised him that I would come up with the money by that Friday (which also happened to be our wedding anniversary), and I would take my sons and leave Houma and Louisiana for good!

Twenty-Four

Lettie brought the boys and I home and promised she would see what she could come up with to help me. But the Lord had given me the assurance that everything had already been taken care of. Butch informed me he was scheduled to get his check that Thursday after work. I told him that I was sorry that things had not been working out for us lately, and I wanted to plan a special anniversary dinner for us that Friday, but I needed the car in order to get everything.

Butch finally agreed and said that I could take him to work on Friday and keep the car. He said that he would sign his check over to me so I could buy everything for our "special night." During the rest of the week, I packed our clothes while the boys took their naps or at night after Butch did his usual thing—passed out on the couch from drinking. Because Butch watched everything I did like a hawk, after packing the trunk and suitcases I had to put them back where they had been, sometimes on the top shelf in the closet. God was truly with me!

Friday finally came, the boys and I got up very early so we wouldn't make Butch late and cause him to change his mind. When we got to his job, he got out of the car without giving me his check.

He said maybe he should rethink his decision; my heart skipped a few beats as I waited for him to make up his mind. Butch's foreman drove into the parking lot and parked right next to us. When he got out of the car, he told Butch he wanted to talk to him, so he hurriedly signed the check and gave it to me. I was so excited I had to remind myself to slow down and not get a ticket. The kids and I went to the bank to cash the check and told the teller that we only wanted to deposit $200 dollars from the $3,500 check. She gave me the cash, and we headed to the courthouse. I met with the judge and the district attorney and paid the amount he requested, got a receipt, and agreed again to leave the parish as soon as possible.

Next we went to the bus station and purchased tickets for the trip to the train station in New Orleans and for the train ride home to Illinois. The boys didn't understand everything that was going on but the oldest one; Alton commented that I looked happy. I am sure he was expressing this because he so seldom had seen me happy. The kids and I went to the store to purchase everything I would need to feed Butch and get him drunk. I knew that whenever he got drunk, he would beat me, but I promised myself that it would be the very last time he touched me.

I brought the boys McDonald's (their favorite) and got them ready for bed while I cooked the "special dinner." I fixed T-bone steaks smothered with mushrooms and onions (his favorite), baked potatoes with sour cream, salad, and Brown 'n Serve rolls. For desert, I fixed strawberry shortcake with whipped cream. I bought candles and flowers for the table, wineglasses, a couple of bottles of his favorite wine (Boone's Farm ☺), and, of course, Budweiser beer. I tried to find something special to wear, but since I wasn't allowed to buy many dress-up clothes for myself, I did not have much to choose from. I wore a pantsuit, which I dressed up with a scarf.

I ran Butch a hot bubble bath and laid out his smoking jacket. His cousin brought him home from work. After taking his bath and getting dressed, I announced that dinner was served. He loved everything; we toasted each other and the boys, and because I was pregnant, he allowed me to turn down the wine and beer and drink a 7UP. He kept telling me that everything was perfect and that he was sorry for treating me so badly and that everything was going to be better from now on. I found myself falling for his beautiful words and wondering if maybe I should change my mind and stay.

Well, that thought was short-lived because I said something that he didn't like, and he started hitting me upside my head. By the time he finished, and we had "sex" (I know now that it was actually rape) since I never agreed to it. He passed out on the couch naked. It was about 5:00 a.m. when he finally drifted off into his usual comatose state. I started gathering the suitcases and trunk and placed them on the porch. Next I got the boys up, washed them up, and dressed them. They quietly ate breakfast (as not to wake up Daddy)! I remembered I needed to call a cab; during our "romantic dinner" Butch informed me that the phone had been cut off. Butch had taken back his keys when he got home and hid them, and I remembered the closest public phone was about one and a half miles away, and I did not have time to walk that distance. My only other option was my next-door neighbor (remember the groupie for the KKK)!

I knocked on her door, and after unlocking what seemed like ten locks, she opened the door and asked me what I was doing on her porch. I explained that I had an emergency and needed to use her phone. Now I really didn't expect her to just open up her door and let me in, so I was prepared to knock her on her bony behind and use her phone. She told me that she didn't allow niggers in her house, let alone use a phone; after all, she would have to burn it if I used it! I got real close to her "good" ear and told her, "I going to use your phone today, and if it has to be over your dead body, so be it." I didn't know an old woman could move that fast; she just started pointing at her phone on the coffee table. After I had called the cab company, I laid a $1 bill beside the phone and thanked her.

On my way home I prayed that Butch hadn't woke up, and thank God, I found him still asleep—passed out—on the couch. When the cab came, I asked the driver to please load our luggage into his trunk, and I buckled the boys in the backseat. I told the driver that I had one last thing to do, and I would be right back, he replied, "It's your dime." I went back into the house and looked at the poor excuse of a man I had called my husband for five long years. After a few moments of reflecting I climbed up on the top of the back of the couch and kicked his narrow behind off! He woke up he asked me if had I lost my mind, and I replied, "No, I'm going home." I then went outside and got into the taxi.

I told the driver to leave, and he started backing out of the drive. I was crying tears of joy so hard that I did not see what the boys and the cab driver saw: My husband was running toward the cab, naked as the day he was born, yelling! I thought he was saying, "Come back, I love you!" Or at least, "Bring back my sons." But all he said was, "Bring back my money, bitch."

After arriving at the bus station I realized that I had twenty minutes before our bus arrived to load! Butch had time to get to the bus station since Houma was so small. The boys and I sat down by our luggage, and I closed my eyes for the first time in what seemed like days! God spoke to my spirit and assured me that Butch would not find us!

The boys and I took the bus to the train station and checked our bags. I just kept thinking, *We're almost home!* We boarded the train and found our seats, we would have to sit in seats during the trip, I didn't want to spend the money on sleeping quarters. I noticed an elderly Caucasian lady was sitting across from our seats (thank goodness, no one was scheduled for the empty seat in our group of four seats). She seemed nice enough and smiled when our eyes met. Then suddenly she looked like she had seen a ghost! I asked her if she were okay, and she said she was. Later I found out why she had reacted the way she had.

We had been riding for a couple of hours and the boys (ages three and four) had taken a nap and wanted to see what else was on the train since it was our first time riding one. I had been trying to rest my eyes, I was so tired, but I started to get up to take them to the dining car when the elderly lady touched my arm. I was surprised and wondered if I had been snoring or the boys had bothered her. But she very quietly told me that she noticed that I was tired and asked if I would mind if she took the boys to the dining car and for a tour of the train. Now of course my first instinct was to tell her no thank you, but again God spoke to my spirit and told me it's okay let her take the boys. She won't hurt them! I looked at the boys, and by that time they were jumping up and down with excitement, so I asked if she was sure and that I would appreciate it. She told me to try and get some rest; she could tell I had been through a lot and felt that I needed a break. I thanked her again, and after they left I decided to go to the bathroom while I had a chance.

On my way to the bathroom I realized just how long it had been since I had actually been to the bathroom! Once I located the women's lounge, I went in and decided that I would splash some water on my face before I used the bathroom. I looked up in the mirror while I was drying my face with the paper towel, and I almost screamed! Now I knew why the taxi driver, the bus driver, the man assisting us with our luggage on the train, and the kind lady who took the boys so I could rest were all staring at! Half of my face was bruised so bad that my right eye was barely open, and I looked like I hadn't been to a hairdresser in years! I hadn't looked in the mirror in so long, I guess I was depending on Butch to tell me how I looked. I hadn't had my hair done since I was in Rockford for the reunion and had just been pulling it back into a ponytail or bun. I wondered why my sons hadn't said anything about how I looked, but it dawned on me that they were used to seeing me look like this!

Butch did not come after us as I feared; surprisingly he finally did a decent thing and let the boys and I go. It took us a while to get to Union Station in Chicago. But thank God we finally arrived! I give God all of the credit for our escape from one of Satan's angels. Thank God my mother was at the station waiting for us as she promised. Of course, my sons were excited to see their grandmother, but all I could do was cry when I saw the expression she had when she saw my face. After we got everything loaded in the car and the boys fastened in their seat belts in the backseat, we took off heading west to the city that would be our home for the next several years!

Twenty-Five

After we reached my mother's house, we took everything out of the car and placed it in the living room and put the boys to bed. Thank goodness, we had stopped and eaten on the way home, so that was one less thing I had to take care of before I lay down. Mama and I discussed where the children and I would stay. We realized staying with her was not realistic, not only because she really didn't have the room, but also because the state would include her income when considering me for public aid assistance.

My grandmother on my father's side and I weren't close, but she respected me and loved the kids. Mama Mae had an apartment in the basement of her house that she rented out to couples or individuals who want more privacy than the room for rent would offer. There was a small kitchen, a little sitting area for a small table and chairs, a small room that was large enough for a set of bunk beds, a shower stall, and a larger room with a double bed. I didn't relish the idea of staying with my grandmother, but I thanked her and God for providing a roof over my family's head, which had to be my main concern.

There was a single man living in the apartment already, but he agreed to move upstairs to the guest room. I told my grandmother that I really appreciated her allowing us to move in and promised that I would do my best to keep the boys quiet as not to disturb her. We agreed on an amount, and my mother (bless her heart) found me some bunk beds for the boys, a small table, and chairs. My mother worked as a supervisor at Goodwill, and she got first look at the donations that came in. Those donations were a godsent for me and the children during the time my mother worked there.

It was difficult living in Mama Mae's basement. It was damp, and as everything else in her house, it smelled like mothballs! I hated mothballs, always had—that is, until my current husband told me that they kept snakes away and kept clothes from getting holes in them. But I still could have lived without them! The boys and I walked to the park a lot to get out of the house. I even ran into some people that I had known since I was a child. One man in particular was Mr. Perteete. He had been a member of the church I grew up in Providence Baptist Church and was one of the sweetest people I had ever met. Mr. Perteete was known for predicting the sex of a child (back then we didn't have ultrasounds).

He told me that I was going to have a girl, I was very pleased and thanked him, and I also knew that if he was wrong about the sex, he would give me a fifty-cent piece! More confirmation came a few days later when the boys and I were shopping at the local grocery store. I had seen this man around our city for quite a while, but I had never had a conversation with him before. He approached me and said, "Little sister, you are going to have a girl, and you should name her Emtesha."

Well, needless to say, I was happy about hearing his prediction, but I told him I don't know anything about him, so why would I let him name my child? He told me that my daughter would be very beautiful and the name *Emtesha* meant "enchanted flower" in the African language. Now I didn't know if this was true, but I felt something when he talked to me! I thanked him and continued doing my shopping. Of course I couldn't help but remember the name, and when she was born, I named her Emtesha Simone (after Nina Simone the singer). I met Ms. Simone at NIU when she came to speak along with Rev. Jesse Jackson. The words she spoke were about having a positive self-image regardless of what others thought about you. Little did I know at the time that her words would be very comforting to me later in my life! Nina was not known for her outward beauty, but if you ever met her and talked to her, you would know that her inner beauty and wisdom were the only thing that you saw once you met her.

My mother allowed me to take her to work one day and keep the car, the kids stayed with my grandmother, and I was able to go to the Department of Public Aid and sign up for assistance. I have never seen myself on public assistance, but it had been there when I needed it, and I felt blessed to have the help. Mama also picked us up every Sunday morning and took us to her new church, Miles Memorial CME. I had visited there when I came for the reunion, and I enjoyed the services. Mama played the piano, and I really enjoyed hearing the boys sing in the children's choir. I also couldn't help but notice that despite everything the boys were really happy!

I contacted a law office that assisted women on public aid and others with below-poverty income file for divorce. My attorney was a young female, and she was wonderful! She informed me that I could start on the paperwork, but I would not be granted a divorce until my child was born. I told her I understood. I needed to be married when the baby was born so Butch would legally be responsible. I gave her the information she needed to file the petition, but when she asked me about child support, I started laughing uncontrollably! She asked me to explain why that was so funny, but when I shared some more of my history with Butch, she said that she understood. We decided that we would not deal with support right now, she said that I could petition for it later, she realized that I just wanted freedom for my sons, the baby, and myself.

I was awarded public assistance in the form of food stamps, a medical card for the children and myself, and a check every month. You can't begin to imagine the joy that I felt when I got my first envelope with my assistance. This was the first money that I was able to say was mine in years. I praised God until I was hoarse, my boys seemed to understand my joy and praised God with me, and even the baby started kicking!

We stayed with my grandmother without incident; she even seemed to enjoy having us around! Then something happened, I killed White Boy. Maybe I should clarify. I took one of her cat's nine lives! My grandmother loved cats, she always had one, and they had the complete run of the house. Now I don't like cats, and if we had a pet when we were kids, it was always a dog and named him Spot, after the dog that Dick and Jane had in our grade-school readers (I know I am really dating myself)! Anyway, the boys had taken their showers and gone to bed, so I decided to go upstairs and take a bubble bath (it had been so long)! My mistake was in leaving the basement door cracked so I could hear the boys if they needed me. I soaked for about a half hour, listening to music and relaxing. I got out when I noticed that I was starting to wrinkle up like a prune. I looked forward to having a good-night's sleep. I had accomplished so much in the short time I had been there and finally decided I could relax and enjoy my new life! I dried off got into my gown and got into bed. I had just started drifting off to sleep when I got this feeling that someone or something was watching me. I opened my eyes and looked right into two bright green ones! I started screaming and instinctively reached out and grabbed at whatever it was and flung it against the wall. Well, White Boy started screeching and hollering like someone had killed him; well, I guess you could say I did!

My grandmother raced down the stairs yelling, "What did you do to White Boy? What did you do to my baby?"

I tried to explain what happened, but she wasn't hearing it. Needless to say, my days at Mama Mae's house were numbered!

Twenty-Six

I got busy with my search for a new home for my growing family, since Emtesha was due in a couple of months! I sat down and figured out a budget and with the money that I had been able to save and the money I received from public assistance. I realized that I could only afford a place in the projects. Now by no means did I feel that the projects were beneath me and the boys especially after living in a house on stilts! But I had grown up in the same house most of my childhood with the exception of the four months that we spent at the parsonage because of the fire. I just never pictured myself living in the projects! I started putting in applications at both the city and county project offices. I was informed that there were not any openings anywhere. I told them thank you for accepting my applications and began praying to the only one who could make this happen for us!

God answered my prayer a lot sooner than I expected, although I always knew that God could open doors that no man can open! I had gotten a letter from my doctor that stated due to the advance stage of my pregnancy and all the trauma that I had experienced since her conception (and before), I needed to move as soon as possible. The doctor also wanted me to be in my own place before I delivered.

With God's intervention and the letter from the doctor, I was able to move the following week into our new home! My mother and Goodwill came to my rescue again, another sign of God's mercy and goodness. He is such an awesome God, and I felt blessed to be His child! My mother found me a beautiful set of living room furniture; the couch and two chairs were a moss green velvet and had high backs. Later I found a set of tables and a large room-size rug at the local Salvation Army store. I felt like I had moved into a mansion. Our apartment had three bedrooms and a bathroom upstairs and a living room and kitchen downstairs. We were so grateful for our new home and everything that God had blessed us with! God had delivered us out of our Egypt and brought us to our promise land—Blackhawk Projects, which is part of Rockford Housing Authority.

I continued to be blessed in the form of my neighbors. I met a wonderful woman next door with two boys and two girls. She was a Christian and often invited me to her church. Her oldest daughter became my babysitter on those rare occasions that I was able to go somewhere in the evening. She was the sweetest young lady, and the children loved her. Later I will tell you how this supposedly sweet young lady ended up being one of my worst enemies. My experiences in Blackhawk were very eye-opening. My neighbor two doors down also became a very good friend. Vera had two boys and a daughter. The boys were the only ones regularly still living with her; her daughter was there occasionally. She worked at Eagle's food store and was a very beautiful person inside and out. My children became her grandchildren, and we spent a lot of time over to her house; her sons took Alton and Tony outside and played basketball and football with them. I was so happy that they had some very nice older boys to watch over them. I loved sharing with Vera. She was like an older sister to me, one who was very wise and sweet. She would often bring home fruit and baked goods for the children and me, and she refused to accept any money in return. When Jackie was not available to watch the children, Vera would insist they spend the night with the boys.

I delivered Emtesha at Rockford Memorial Hospital with my mother by my side; my brother Dennis was at mama's house watching the boys. I should back up a bit and tell you about the winter of

1978 and 1979. This was one of the worst winters that Rockford had experienced, and I was very pregnant. All advanced pregnant women were encouraged by the police to check themselves into the hospital as soon as possible. I wasn't about to leave my sons and go into the hospital a month ahead of my due date; plus it was almost Christmas. So my mother convinced me and the boys to move in with her until I delivered. The boys loved living with Grandma and Uncle Dennis. I, on the other hand, missed my privacy. But when I think back on my situation, how much privacy do you need when you are eight-months-plus pregnant with two young children. Anyway, I talked my mother into fixing my favorite meal after reminding her of the food at the hospital that I would have to endure soon. We had chitterlings, spaghetti, coleslaw, and fried chicken.

While the food was cooking I decided to make sure my suitcase contained everything I needed for my delivery. Well, I started having some pains—maybe labor pains, maybe not. At this point I really did not want to know. I was smelling dinner and was determined to eat! About an hour later I was fixing my plate, you have to understand this is my very favorite food, and there is no way that I was going to miss it. So, I started eating, and, of course, everything was wonderful. I had just finished tasting a little bit of everything when I got this sharp pain. I stood up and grabbed my stomach. My mother asked if I was in labor. I looked at the food and lied, "No, Mama, not yet."

Well, I continued eating, and after I had finished my second helping, I admitted that yes, I was in labor, and the pains were about six minutes apart! My mother gave me this look and told my brother to call 911. I was used to my mother going off on me, like the time I came home from a date at 2:00 a.m. because I was to be eighteen years old in two weeks and thought I was grown. But this time she shot daggers through me with her eyes. I just kind of dropped my head and grabbed my aching stomach, hoping she would have mercy on me. The ambulance arrived about fifteen minutes later, and after strapping me in, I stopped crying out long enough to request lights and sirens (this had always been a private fantasy of mine). By the time we arrived at the hospital, my mother was coming out of the emergency room looking for us.

Emtesha's delivery was the hardest that I had had so far. Also, because I had eaten so much food, I had an accident on the doctor and nurses! I tried to apologize but sorry didn't quite make up for the crap that they had on them! Anyway the boys were a piece of cake compared to delivering Emtesha. The most important thing that I thank God for was for the size of Emtesha! I thought because I had missed so many meals, the baby would be smaller and therefore easier to deliver. But we serve an awesome God, and Emtesha was the largest of all four of my children. I was so thankful that my mother was able to stay at the hospital with me. I gained so much strength from her presence. Emtesha was born on January 17, 1979, after about eight hours of intense labor.

Twenty-Seven

After we were discharged from the hospital we went back to my mom's house for a few weeks, so by the time we were able to go home, the kids and I were more than ready. Emtesha was a few days old when I decided to make the call and inform her father he was a dad again. I don't know what I expected him to say, but he sounded like he was really happy about her birth and missed the boys and me. I felt myself starting to weaken. I started thinking about how nice it would be to have my family complete again.

I thought, *He sounds so different. Maybe he has changed, and we can make it this time.*

He told me that he was going to come to Rockford as soon as he could get the money together, and he wanted to bring us back to Houma where we could be a happy family again. I started crying and remembering "better times" between us. Now mind you, we didn't have a whole lot of better times to draw from, but he had a way of making me see things through rose-colored glasses.

My mother started telling me to get off the phone, I assured her I would be getting off soon, and she started demanding that I get off now! I told Butch my mom was tripping and I would call him back later. My mother stopped what she was doing and sat down next to me.

She said, "I didn't want to have to tell you this, but I think it's something you should hear now!"

My mom went on to ask if I remembered the day that my oldest son Alton was born. I told her of course I did. Butch and I were together, and we were so happy. I asked Mama why she felt the need to bring this up now, and she told me that after Butch left the hospital he went home to our apartment.

I said, "Yeah, what about it?"

She reminded me that she left later that evening and went by the apartment on her way home. Now I was really anxious to hear what she had to say. Mama said that as she passed the house, she saw my husband (the same one who had just left the hospital an hour prior) getting out of our car with his whore! Mama said she sat there and watched them enter into our apartment building holding hands! I just sat there and cried. At first, I didn't want to believe her, but after thinking about it, I realized that it sounded just like something he would do. I called Butch back and asked him about the incident. I don't know what I expected him to say, but he did not disappoint me. He lied of course!

My divorce was final on April 1, 1979. I had been given full and sole custody of my three children; I had officially been set free of Butch! At the same time I recognized that I was unemployed, and I was totally responsible for the care of my children and myself. My first car after leaving Butch was a Ford Pinto. I was surprised to find out that I could afford this cute blue car! I was so excited to finally have my own car that I failed to check it out completely. It started, and that was my only requirement until I found out that there was a problem with the floor on the front passenger's side. The guy that sold it to me "forgot" to mention that there really wasn't a floor on the passenger's side. I found out one evening while I was taking the children over to my best friend's house for an evening of movies and eating. My best friend Lizzie was like no one I have ever known before or since. She was a divorcee with one son. Her son was older than mine, but they were best friends especially when he allowed them to play with his big-boy toys. Lizzie said he loved having someone younger around so he could play big-brother to them.

This particular night I had Emtesha in the front seat with her car seat facing the rear of the car. It had been raining that evening, and that part of Central had some very big potholes. Well, that night my Pinto seemed to find the worst of these holes. I had gone through an especially large one, and Emtesha started screaming. I asked Butchie to look over the seat and see why she was crying. He informed me that she was drowning! I pulled over to the side of the road to see what he was talking about and saw that the water from the pothole had come up through the floor and splashed all over her.

My first thought was to laugh. She did look like she was drowning. I hurried and got some of her cloth diapers and dried her the best I could. Thank goodness, we were close to Lizzie's apartment, and I was able to change her into dry clothes. My sons reminded Emtesha constantly that she had "drowned" in our car. My father fixed the floor and checked the rest of the car for me. What was my next move? I was living in Blackhawk Projects, and driving a Pinto with a patched-up floor! I started experiencing bouts of depression and knew that I had to get myself together for my children's sake. I'm not going to say it was easy because it wasn't. I remember quietly crying in my room so I wouldn't wake up the boys in their room and my daughter who was still sleeping in the room with me.

My sister Beverly invited me down to Champaign, Illinois, for my birthday. She said that she had some friends she would invite over, and we would have a party. I know what she was trying to do. I was in a bad way, and my family was concerned that I might go back to Butch. I have to admit that it had crossed my mind. I'm not even sure why. I had spent so much of my adult life with Butch, I was afraid of trying something different especially on my own. Lizzie offered to watch the kids for a week while I went to Champaign. She took a week of vacation time off from her job to stay with my kids. It finally occurred to me that people were really concerned about my state of mind.

Champaign, Illinois, is a very typical college town. U of I is located there and is a very well-known university. My sister worked for DCFS and had two daughters. She was also divorced, only she was receiving child support (something I had never had the privilege of knowing about).

The party was wonderful. I got a chance to meet some of Beverly's friends and some of their friends, especially Lonnie. Lonnie had heard about the party and came over to meet me. I was instantly attracted to him; he was very handsome and had dimples. We got to know each other that night while doing the "Bump" to Reunited by Peaches and Herb. I have always been able to learn all of the latest dances and know all of the latest music, so of course, I had a wonderful time. For the first time in my adult life I forgot about all of my responsibilities and just enjoyed myself, if only for a little while.

Lonnie and I became quite an item; he was a junior at U of I and a biology major. Lonnie came to Rockford about two times a month; he would stay with my girlfriend's boyfriend a few miles from my apartment. My next-door neighbor's daughter was still babysitting for me whenever I got a chance to go to the movies or out to dinner. It worked out well for both of us, she loved getting a few dollars to buy clothes, and I was able to get an occasional break. Well, one Friday night after Lonnie and I had gone out to dinner, we decided to return home earlier than usual to watch movies at home. We walked in and caught Jackie (my sweet innocent babysitter) and her nappy-headed boyfriend getting it on on my green velvet couch! Of course, I went ballistic and told her to get the hell out of my house, and she had the nerve to stop at the door and ask for the money she felt I owed her. I grabbed her neck and took her back to the couch and told her she owed me for using my couch. Needless to say she never kept the kids again. I dated a couple of other guys after Lonnie, nothing serious, mind you, just occasionally going out for dinner or a movie when my sister Charisse was available.

Twenty-Eight

During that time the only thing that saved me was the work that I did at church. I became a Sunday school teacher, a youth director, and I was the financial secretary for our church, Miles Memorial C.M.E. The kids and I were at the church at least three times a week. The children were good friends with the other kids at the church, and one of my good friends Marcy joined the church and assisted me with the youth department. Things were going as well as I could have expected. My best friend Lizzie was also a member of Miles Memorial, and even though she was divorced from her husband, she was still close to his parents, and his father just happened to be our pastor at the time. My mother was the musician, and the kids sung in the children's choir.

My sister Charisse started coming by to hang out with me and the kids. At that time we were both obsessed with the movie *The Rose* starring Bette Midler. We would sit and sing the theme song of the movie over and over again. My kids still tease me about it, and I remind them that there are worst things than being obsessed with a movie. The children loved hanging out with Charisse; she loved coloring and playing games with them. I also loved having Charisse over. It was nice to talk to a grown-up after dealing with three kids all day.

I should have stuck with enjoying Charisse's company instead of becoming involved with my second husband, Joe Hughes. My son Tony was playing basketball for Blackhawk Projects in their gym, and Charisse offered to watch Emtesha while Alton and I went to the game to watch Tony play. Their team was playing against Washington Park Community Center, which was from my old neighborhood. Washington Park won the game by two points, but Tony made a couple of baskets and was happy that he was able to play. We were about to walk back to the apartment when someone tapped me on my shoulder. I turned and saw Joe. I had not seen him in over ten years. I had gone off to NIU, and he had gone to Vietnam as a US Marine. We started catching up, and he ended up walking us home. Charisse remembered him, and we sat around and talked about the good old days on the west end.

Joe had two older brothers who had gone to school with my older siblings and a younger sister who was around Charisse's age. We actually grew up around the corner from each other. I had a mild crush on him when we were in middle school and was too shy at the time to tell him. Joe had the sexiest smile; he had a gap in the front that made him look younger when he smiled. All of those old feelings came back as we got reacquainted. Joe was one of the coaches of the basketball team at Washington Park and said that he had been working there for a couple of years.

I was so excited about the possibility of a relationship with him, especially since he was someone whom I thought I knew from back in the day, someone I felt I could trust. Joe spent most of his free time with the children and I, and we became a family. I loved having someone in my life whom I felt would never hurt me like Butch had. I shared my history with him. I told him what Butch had put me and the boys through. I told him that I thought Butch was going to kill me and how frightened I had been almost the entire time we were together. Joe kept reassuring me that he would never ever treat me like that. He said he would always treat me with respect and devotion. He said he wanted to take care of me and the kids and make sure that we wanted for nothing. He admitted that he had also had a crush on me when we were in school and didn't think I would have given him the time of day. We were together whenever he wasn't working or I wasn't at church.

Joe proposed marriage, and after I accepted, he informed me that we needed special permission to get married. He went on to explain that because I was divorced, the elder of his church had to approve of our union as they did not condone divorces. We met with Elder Talley, and I explained the circumstances surrounding my divorce from Butch. It helped that the elder's children and I attended school together, and he knew my parents.

Our marriage was approved, and the "special rules" of the church were explained to me. Let me explain: Women were not allowed to wear pants ever! Opened-toe shoes were frowned upon, women were to never enter the church without having something covering their heads, and, last but not least, women were not supposed to smoke; however, men could. I didn't like the "rules," but I loved Joe and was willing to make the necessary adjustments. Our wedding was very unusual to say the least. My sister Beverly was my maid of honor, and Joe's brother was his best man. Butchie and Tony were ring bearers, and Emtesha was the flower girl. This part was normal enough. However, the attitudes of the older women were constantly getting on my nerves. My family and friends were not used to the "covering of the head" rule and arrived at the church to decorate or practice without coverings. I told them to just hold a Kleenex over their head. This did not go over well! Some of the elderly women would just "show up" whenever we were there and sit and talk about us until we left.

When it came to the reception, we decided to just have my friends bring food instead of gifts. I thought it was a good idea; however, "the women of the church" interfered with everything my friends arrived with and caused a lot of problems. This should have been a red flag waving, but I kept saying, "It's all good." Or, "It's going to be all right."

Finally, the day arrived, and we were married. We spent our "honeymoon" at the Wagon Wheel Lodge not far from Rockford. Well, maybe I should rephrase that, I spent our honeymoon night watching my husband get drunk at a party our friends threw for us, and after arriving at the hotel, I listened to him snore!

Twenty-Nine

Joe moved in to my apartment in Blackhawk when we first got married. When we could afford it, we went out to dinner or the drive-in, and I reluctantly got my old babysitter to watch the kids when we went out. Big mistake, real big mistake! One Friday night while at the drive-in, we saw an advertisement for a newly renovated hotel on East State Street in Rockford. They advertised a special deal offering a "mirrored" room (mirrors on the ceiling and the walls) for a discounted price. We laughed and talked about going there one day just for the fun of it. After the movie, Joe surprised me by driving to a 7-Eleven and purchasing toothbrushes and other necessities for us, got back in the car, and announced that we were going to the hotel! I immediately reminded Joe that my diaphragm was at home, and he promised to withdraw before it was too late. Well, nine months later my fourth child, Melan'ie, was the result of his "withdraw"! I have never had morning sickness with any of my children, and this pregnancy was no exception. Joe was thrilled with the idea of having a little Joe running around. I spent most of the nine months reminding him that having a son was not something either of us could control.

BACK TO THE BEGINNING

Not long after I got pregnant the arguments started, first just small things like him not coming directly home from work. Shortly after that, they excelled to him coming home all times of the night drunk. Now mind you, the whole time we were dating I never saw Joe drunk. Oh, he had an occasional beer now and then but never to excess. I suspected that he was fooling around, but of course, he would always deny it. Then one day I saw just how much his drinking was affecting him. I had taken the children to Blackhawk Day Care and returned home to find Joe at the apartment. Joe worked during the day at the center, and I wondered why he was home so early. After I asked, he told me that he had gotten into a little trouble and was suspended for a few days. I asked what happened and immediately realized that was the wrong thing to do. He started yelling at me and reminding me that I wasn't his mama and could not question him!

Joe knew that I wanted to start working, and he mentioned that there might be a job for me at Washington Park Center as a day care director. I got my résumé together and submitted it to Mr. Davis. I immediately liked his professional but nice manner. Mr. Davis informed me that the person hired would be working for the Rockford Park District. He also informed me that the person would have to be able to qualify to direct a day care center using the rules and regulations established by DCFS. I met with the necessary people and found out that with my degree in elementary education and the classes that I took in early childhood development, I would more than qualify. I was hired and given a list of my responsibilities. Since I was going to be the first person to be director, I had to recommend people to hire and buy everything from baby beds to children toys. I enjoyed looking through catalogs picking out different things that I knew my children liked at different stages. The area that we would use for the day care was painted, and new carpet was laid. I had my own office, which I didn't intend to spend a lot of time in. I wanted to be a hands-on director.

After the day care opened, my youngest Emtesha was able to come to work with me, which was a huge help. Emtesha was a very friendly child and quickly made friends with several of the center's children. I enrolled the boys in my old elementary school, William Dennis, which was in walking distance. Everything seemed to be coming together. Joe and I argued less. Since we were both working at the same place, we agreed to keep things civil at least at work. I was very pregnant by this time, and everyone at work was excited about the baby. Some of the ladies I worked with gave me a baby shower. It was the first one after having three kids! We got some very nice gifts. Most of them were yellow or mint green because back then we didn't have ultrasounds to determine the baby's sex. Therein was the problem for Joe who kept asking where all the blue boy's clothes were. He was still holding on to the hope that we would have a boy. I learned to just let him hope all he wanted to and not to disagree with him; that was one less thing to argue about.

All hell broke loose one night when Joe had gone out for one of his "dates" with my ex-babysitter—yes, my old babysitter! Anyway I had gone to bed because I had started getting headaches due to stress, and I just wanted to get some sleep while he was out. I left the chain off the door so he could stumble in when he came home like I usually did if I went to bed early. I woke up when I heard the door being slammed and wondered if someone had broken in. I looked around our bedroom trying to find something to use to protect myself when in walked Joe. I asked him why he slammed the door (I forgot not to question him). He started cursing at me and saying I should have remembered to put the chain back on after my "boyfriend" had left. I asked him what he was talking about.

"I left the chain off for you!"

That was the last thing I remembered saying before the right side of my face got introduced to the headboard of our bed. Now we had a very decorative headboard. It had a lot of designs in it, and ordinarily I really loved it, but when I finally woke up and went to the bathroom and saw the imprint of the headboard on the right side of my face, I decided that we should have gotten a plain one.

I had to go to work the next day, and there was no way that makeup would cover up the imprint. I got dressed and tried to explain to the children that I had an accident, but I was fine now. The looks I got from Butchie and Tony let me know they weren't believing one word I was saying. I had to be at work earlier than Joe, so I left him in bed while the kids and I made our way to the day care. When I got to work I made sure the boys got off to school, and I was glad that some friends of theirs had stopped by the center to walk to school with them. Maybe they could keep their minds off of what they saw this morning. I saw a lot of people pretending not to stare and heard lots of whispering behind my back, which I had expected. I went into my office and closed the door, but as soon as I picked up the phone, one of my coworkers came in and asked if I was all right. I told her not yet but I would be fine soon. She looked at me and said, "Okay, let me know if you need me."

I called the police and told them what happened, and they asked if I wanted them to go to our apartment and pick him up, and I said no. I heard the officer sigh, and I thought he must think I'm not going to press charges like so many other battered woman. But I informed him that I wanted Joe arrested at his job, which was also where I happened to work, so I could sign the complaint when they arrived to get him. It took about forty-five minutes for the police to arrive. I knew that it would take a while because they never answered calls quickly on that side of town. Joe arrived at work and changed into his sweats and then went into the gym as he usually did, and just as he was asking about joining a basketball game, the police walked in!

Perfect timing, all of his friends from the hood saw him being arrested and having handcuffs put on his wrist. He had the nerve to be shocked. I guess he didn't remember me telling him no one else was going to hit me and get away with it!

Thirty

We moved into our new home the first day of May 1982. I was very, very pregnant and was ready to have it. We ended up moving into a home in our old neighborhood, the house belong to Elder Talley from our church, and it was located in the middle of our parents' home's literally! By this time Joe was working at the Byron Nuclear Plant, and I assumed he was making good money. I had to assume this because unbeknown to me, Joe gave his checks to "his mommy dearest," and she paid all of his bills. When we became husband and wife, Joe informed me that whenever I started working, he would be taking my checks to his mother also, and she would handle our affairs. After all of the years of abuse from Butch, not having any kind of say so over anything, and being controlled by him, I wasn't about to give my check to anyone! Joe said he was very disappointed in me and his mother would be also. I gave him a look that displayed my true feelings, and he left to go see his mother. His mother also didn't like the idea that I was a divorced woman with three children. I don't think she counted on us getting married in the first place, and when that worked out, she thought the "rules of the church" would stop us from getting married.

My next surprise came the first Sunday that Joe and I went to church as a couple. I could deal with the no-pants rule and even wearing something on my head every time I went to church, but whoever heard of the men sitting on the right side of the church and the women sitting on the left side? Well, I immediately broke that rule and sat myself next to my husband each Sunday that he attended. I was the only woman on the right side, and I created quite a stir! Thank goodness, the children attended children's church in the building next door and missed the ugly stares that their mother was getting. Joe's church also did not believe in women wearing makeup or nail polish. I never was a big fan of makeup, and I couldn't afford to get my nails done, so that was no big deal, but whenever I asked a question regarding the doctrine that we were studying, I was told to ask my husband.

Now I was raised to believe that the husband is the head of the household, and I agreed with that in principle, but when I found out that Joe intended to attend church only on holidays, asking him questions seemed ridiculous! He could only tell me to ask his mother, so that was out of the question since we only spoke when necessary. I was happy that I became acquainted with some of the young ladies around my age, and even though they were related to Joe, they were nothing like his mother, so we got along great.

I was so tired of being pregnant I started trying to find things that would force me into labor like cutting the grass with a push mower. I did that for a couple of weeks, and the next thing, I knew I went into labor; however, I would never suggest anyone try that method of speeding up delivery. I had very bad back pains during labor. We dropped the children off at my mother's house, by this time my brother was away at school, so Mama couldn't come with us. I didn't realize how hard it would be to be in labor without Mama. The only other time she wasn't with me was when Tony was born in Houston, Texas, but I had a spinal and didn't feel anything anyway! I kept trying to reassure myself that my husband was going to be with me, but it didn't seem to comfort me. About two hours later I realized why I had that feeling. I was having contractions every ten minutes and would grab Joe's hand and squeeze it. I thought he understood that me grabbing him was his part of the labor process! But I was wrong. After about two hours, Joe said, "I'm going downstairs to have a cigarette. I'll be back soon."

Well, I don't know what he learned in school, but I was taught what soon meant a few minutes or maybe enough time to smoke a couple of cigarettes. Obviously Joe thought differently, because he never returned! I lay there asking the nurse to page my husband because he must have gotten lost. I couldn't think of any other reason for him not being by my side.

I had been in hard labor for around eight hours when I asked the doctor what I could do to speed this up. I found myself trying to figure out how to get our lawn mower up to the maternity ward! The doctor told me that the baby was in distress and was having a difficult time moving into the birth canal. I asked why he couldn't just do a C-section and remove the baby. I didn't have a problem with having a scar across my stomach! The doctor said that they really didn't want to do that unless it was absolutely necessary; after eight hours of hard labor, I felt that the necessity had arrived! The doctor explained that the baby was lodged in my right side, and every time she tried to move into the canal, she would slip back into my side. He asked if I had slept on my right side the entire time I was pregnant, and I immediately replied yes (that was the best way to stay far away from Joe)! I didn't know what to say; this was all my fault!

I called my mother and told her what was going on and that Joe had left to have a cigarette about seven hours ago and hadn't found his way back to the maternity ward. I was shocked to hear some of the words that came out of my mother's mouth, but I couldn't disagree with the way she was feeling. Since it was in the middle of the night, she couldn't think of anyone to keep the children so she could come to the hospital, and I told her not to worry. I would be okay alone. Just as soon as I hung up the phone, the nurse walked in because the shift had changed, and she was coming in to introduce herself and see how I was doing. I was so happy to see Daisy, she was from my neighborhood, and I had gone to school with one of her sisters. After explaining that Joe was missing in action and none of my family was available to be with me, Daisy told me that she wouldn't leave me even if her shift ended. I don't know how she worked it out with the other staff, but Daisy was in my room constantly; she held my hand and prayed with me. I thanked Daisy and God for her being there with me. I finally delivered Mela'nie at 10:06 a.m. the next day, and I told the doctor in the delivery room I wanted my tubes tied as soon as possible. I had no intention of going through this again! Mela'nie was a beautiful baby with a head full of big, soft curls.

I debated rather to call Joe or not. I really didn't think that he deserved to know, but Daisy encouraged me to try to call him for the baby's sake. I finally called Joe's job and asked for his supervisor. When he came to the phone, I explained the situation and asked if he could tell Joe that his child had been born, and he had a beautiful daughter. His boss called Joe to the phone and asked him why the hell he was at work while his wife was delivering his child. I heard him telling Joe to punch out and go see about his family! It was about two hours later when I received two dozen red roses, and I thought how nice it was for Joe to send me flowers as a way of making up, but after reading the card, I found out that his supervisor had sent the flowers! Joe finally showed up saying he had to go get cleaned up. All I smelled was beer. I guess he was trying out a new cologne! Of course Joe showed up empty-handed and mad. He asked me why I didn't have a boy and then had the nerve to ask me if she was really his!

The nurse brought the baby in when I buzzed her, and Joe took one look at her and said, "She is beautiful, and she's mine. She has the same small hole in her earlobe." Well, thank goodness, this "she isn't mine" stuff was over.

Mela'nie and I went home a few days after she was born, and I immediately wished I could go back to the hospital or Mama's house or anywhere else! Joe hadn't cleaned up since I left, dishes were everywhere, and the bed looked like he had slept in it with his boots on. I just stood there and cried while Joe asked me what I was going to do about his dinner, and then I realized he thought I was like the women during slavery time who squatted down, had their babies, threw them on their back, and kept picking cotton!

Thirty-One

My job at Washington Park Day Care wasn't full-time (that way they would not have to give me benefits), so I had to get back to work after just two weeks so I could have my own money and not rely on Joe's mother. Actually I did have some money. I had been receiving checks from public aid for my older three kids. Joe was not responsible for Alton, Tony, and Emtesha, so I kept receiving a medical card for them and occasionally food stamps and a small check. One thing I learned after Butch was not to tell my husband about all of my money! I had the checks sent to my mother's house, and I would stop by her house and sign them, and she cashed them and put them in a joint account we had opened. I had really good help at the day care, and they helped me out with anything physical, so I was able to sit most of the time. My only problem was finding someone to take care of Mela'nie for me, the day care would have been perfect, but we only took babies who were six months old, so two weeks wasn't going to cut it. I thought about asking her grandmother (Joe's mom) since she didn't work outside of her home, but I soon decided that I didn't want my daughter spending that much time with someone who didn't care that much for her mother. Finally I was able to talk my cousin Bertha into keeping her at her in home day care. Bertha was also willing to keep the boys because school was out, and I could only take Emtesha to work with me. Thank goodness, the boys had some friends in the Terrace where Bertha lived, so they looked forward to going every day.

Things were going pretty good at home, although we did have a snake incident one night. Joe was "working," so he wasn't home. I had just given the kids their bath and put them to bed, so I went to check on Mela'nie in her bassinet. When I first went into the room, I thought I saw something slithering across the floor by her bassinet, but it moved so fast I thought my eyes were playing tricks on me. I picked up the baby and started to leave the room when I saw the snake coming from under the bed! I started screaming and running. I am terrified of snakes, mice, and several insects, but snakes were at the top of that list. I woke the baby and the other children up, and we all ran to the living room. After a few minutes I got brave enough to go into the kitchen (across from the bedroom) and grab the phone off the hook and called Joe's father. Mr. Hughes had said maybe ten words to me the whole time I'd known him, but that night when he came over and got rid of the snake, we talked and laughed for almost an hour. Of course, that was the last time we exchanged that many words, but I had one cool memory I could share with the kids about Joe's father.

When Mela'nie was around two months, things changed drastically. Joe decided that we needed two dogs in the form of Doberman pinschers. One was red, and we called him Red, and the other was black. I guess you can figure out what his name was. Not a lot of imagination was used when it came to naming them. I argued that animals were a lot of responsibility, and I wondered who was supposed to be responsible for these two giant puppies! Joe said they were his dogs, and he would be responsible for them. Yeah right, if you believe that I got a bridge to sell you! I warned the boys that they would probably be called on to help Joe, and they were cool with it; they had always wanted a dog. The garbage truck ran on Thursday, and we sat the garbage in the garage until it ran so that the dogs wouldn't get in it.

The dogs had pens, so I thought this may work out, until it rained one day and Joe insisted that Red and Blackie needed to go into the garage. You can guess what had happened when we went to check on the dogs after the rain stopped. The dogs had garbage all over the garage floor and stood there trying to look innocent. Joe took the dogs out and told the boys to clean up the garage, I started to protest, but I figured it wouldn't hurt them, and it would be good exercise. But first, I asked Joe if he could put the garbage up on one of the shelves so the dogs couldn't get back in it; he agreed that that would be a good idea and said he would as soon as the boys finished. Well, the boys got through and told Joe he could put the trash up now, but by that time Joe had been drinking and said that he would do it later. I told the boys to wash up so they could eat. I figured it was Joe's problem now.

The next day the kids and I arrived home in the middle of a thunderstorm and immediately noticed that the dogs were not in their pens. I said a small prayer hoping that Joe put the trash up before the rain started. But of course, he hadn't, and as soon as the rain stopped, he took the dogs back out to their pens and told the boys to go and clean up the garage. Before the boys could respond, I told Joe, "Hell no, my sons are not going to clean up after your dogs again." I reminded him that he promised to put the trash up on the shelf so the dogs couldn't reach it.

He said, "Yeah, but I didn't have time, so the boys can go clean up, and then I will put the bags up on the shelf."

I repeated myself and said hell no, my sons aren't touching that mess! Joe insisted that either they pick up the trash, or I could take all my kids and leave "his" house. I told him that we would be out as soon as I could find a place to move to. He looked at me and laughed, saying, "You aren't going anywhere. You don't have any money"! I just stood thinking about the money I had saved and smiled!

I started looking in the newspaper for apartments that evening after dinner. He kept making comments about us not being able to leave "his" house any time soon. God showed me the perfect apartment in my dreams that night, and I knew He would reveal it to me soon, but I only had to wait until the next day! A friend of mine told me that her grandmother had an upstairs apartment that had been vacated unexpectedly, and she wanted to rent it as soon as possible. I made an appointment to go and see the apartment later that day after work. It was perfect; it had three bedrooms and a large kitchen. Her grandmother reminded me that it came unfurnished, and I told her that would not be a problem.

I was told that I could move in that weekend if I wanted to, and I happily agreed. The next morning after I took all of the kids to Bertha and called in to work and told them I needed a couple of days off to move, I went to the bank and switched my money from a savings account to a checking account. Next I went to U-Hall and rented a truck for Saturday and tried to think of some men whom I could ask to help me move who wouldn't charge me a fortune. I picked the kids up got them McDonald's and took them to "Joe's" house so they could start packing up their rooms as soon as they finished eating. Joe was at home, and he asked where his food was, and I told him wherever he could find it; cooking for him was no longer my job since I was instructed to move and take my kids with me. He shook his head as he headed out the door to go to his parents' home to eat. Before he left, he asked me just how long I was going to keep up this game and reminded me that he wasn't giving me one dime to move!

The next day I called the center and asked Richard, one of the supervisors, if he knew any reliable men I could hire to help me move. Richard said he heard about me supposedly moving out but that Joe had told him we really weren't going anywhere. I assured Richard that we were indeed moving Saturday and asked him if he knew where I could get some help. Richard told me that he would be at my house at 8:00 a.m. Saturday with some help. I thanked him and got off the phone to pack.

Saturday finally came, and I took the kids to my mother's house on my way to pick the truck up. I got back to the house at seven thirty and panicked thinking what if Richard and his friends don't come. What was I going to do? It suddenly hit me that I had less faith as an adult than I had as a child and finally listened for the still soft voice I used to look for, and God told me everything had already been worked out. I started looking around the house to see if we were leaving anything (I am a professional packer, I've moved so much), and I noticed this small cast-iron skillet that I never used because it was only big enough to fix one egg and I told myself, *This will be my parting gift to Joe!*

By the time I returned to the living room Richard and three other guys who worked at the center were standing at the front door. I had everything boxed up, taped, and labeled, so the guys grabbed one of the doughnuts I had picked up and started to work.

Everything was on the truck except the living room couch, which just happened to be occupied by my soon-to-be ex-husband. Now the couch and every other piece of furniture was mine before I met Joe, so I felt justified in taking it all. I asked the men to get the couch, and they protested because Joe was their friend. I asked Joe if he had purchased the couch or had I owned it before we met, and, thank goodness, he told the truth and said it was mine, but he wasn't moving.

The guys looked at one another, went over to the couch, picked it up, dumped Joe on the floor, and proceeded to put the couch on the truck. The move went very well, so I felt bad, and I apologized for not having much to pay them. They all refused to take any money from me; they told me they were glad to do it. God did say that everything had been taken care of, and God never lies! I took the truck back and dropped the key in the night slot. Since my mother had agreed to keep the kids all night, I didn't have to worry about them. But when I called her to pick me up, I asked my mom to bring the kids with her, so we could all sleep in *our* new home.

Thirty-Two

The upstairs apartment was a lot bigger then "Joe's" house. The boys loved their large room, which was right off of the kitchen, and so was the girl's room, and by this time Mela'nie was sleeping all night, so she didn't have to sleep in my room any longer. I loved having my room on the other side of the apartment by myself. If any of the kids needed me, I was just a holler away. The apartment was quite a bit farther away from work than the house, so we needed to get up earlier, but none of us minded as long as we were away from Joe and his drinking! One night I was sitting in the living room while the kids played in their rooms, and the baby was in her carrier beside me. I thanked God daily for getting me out of yet another mess, and then I started questioning myself why I picked such losers for husbands. I had been raised in a home without abuse around me, so why was I attracted to men who were abusive? The main conclusion that I reached was that I chose my two husbands, and God had nothing to do with my choices. I had not consulted him on either of my choices!

The job at the day care center was nice, but I needed full-time employment with benefits, so I decided to apply for a position at Goodwill Industries where my mother worked. Her boss asked her if I might be interested in a grant position, and I hesitated because it was funded by a grant. Also, if the program wasn't successful after six months, the funding could be cancelled. I was really interested in the position because it involved working with young teen mothers, and I had already volunteered as a facilitator for a parents-too-soon group at the daycare center in the evenings. I decided to speak to the director of Goodwill and explained my concern regarding the grant. Jon said he completely understood my concern; however, he really wanted to hire me for the position because he had heard about my involvement as a facilitator. I asked if it was possible to guarantee me a year's employment regardless of the grant term. I was surprised when he agreed to put my request in writing, so I gladly took the job.

It was difficult saying good-bye to Mr. Davis and other people at the job, but it was perfect timing because I had just discovered that two of my day care workers were trying to take over the day care center behind my back. I remembered hiring these two young ladies. One didn't have much experience at all, but because I knew her family, I decided to give her a chance. I also found out they had talked to some of the parents to get their help with the takeover. When God closes one door, He opens another; it was time for me to go! Goodwill was close to our new home, and I got the older kids in Blackhawk Day Care, so the boys were taken to school by staff, and Emtesha attended prekindergarten classes at the day care. By that time Mela'nie was a year old, and I found a very nice lady nearby to watch her during the day. Everything was going well, and we were all happy! I noticed that the children were laughing and smiling a lot more. I used to think that the children needed a father in their lives to be happy, but they showed me that we were fine by ourselves. We were regularly attending church again, so we really didn't have any free time to spare. The children were doing wonderful in school, and I was even dating occasionally—nothing serious—and the children never met anyone whom I went out with.

I am so glad that God placed the guarantee in my spirit before I talked to the director because after about seven months, the funding was cancelled. A coworker and I discussed possible reasons why the program was not going well; the person hired to complete the statistical data and submit a quarterly report didn't know what she was doing! You know how it is when someone gets a job because they know someone but haven't got a clue about the job they are asking for? Well, we had such a person in the position, so when the grant ended, she was the first one to go, and the other followed shortly thereafter. I was asked to complete the final statistical report, and since I had taken statistics in college, I agreed. The report was a huge success, and the question was asked: "Why weren't the other reports done by the same person?" God continued to work in my favor when I was asked to complete my year in the evaluation department because of my statistical knowledge! I loved working with Marge; she was around the same age as me and an easy person to talk to. She taught me a lot about evaluating test results and writing reports. Also, while I was in the evaluation department I met some of the counselors from the DORS (the Department of Rehabilitation Services); actually I was able to use two of them as references when I applied for my next job.

Because I had only been guaranteed a year of employment, I started looking for another job about a month before the year was out. Marge said that she wanted to keep me, but they could only hire me part-time. With four children to take care of, I really needed a full-time job! I applied for a position at Illinois Growth Enterprises. Growth, the name everyone that worked there called it, was also a rehabilitation facility like Goodwill. I interviewed with the CEO, the director of Rehabilitation, and some of the board members. I was so nervous answering questions from so many people at one time, but obviously I did okay because I was offered the position of supervisor of a group of twenty-five adults with disabilities. I instantly loved my job not only because I enjoyed working with the clients, but also because I really enjoyed working with my coworkers. I became fast friends with a few of my coworkers; we would eat lunch together and share break times. Growth was a workshop where we assembled, boxed, and shipped parts like hinges and other hardware items. I worked next to my clients instead of instructing them on the job and walking away. The clients weren't used to my method of supervising, but I could tell they liked it by the way they interacted with me. I was told by the other staff that they didn't socialize with the clients outside of work, so I wasn't expected to either. I talked to my supervisor Alan and asked if it was okay to plan a picnic for my group and was given the go-ahead after he gave me a strange look of surprise. I asked the group if they wanted to have the picnic and received the same look of surprise and a loud *yes!*

Everyone chipped in for the food, and one of the older men in the group volunteered to grill the hot dogs and brats. We played baseball, listened to music, and danced. I had left the children with one of my friends, so I had the whole afternoon to spend with my group. Out of the twenty-five people in the group, twenty of them came. Later I found out that the other's parents didn't believe I was actually going to have the picnic! We continued to have outings for the next four years that I was a supervisor.

Thirty-Three

The children and I moved a couple of times after I started working at Growth. I was making a better salary and thought we could afford a better home. We moved on Rose Avenue into a wonderful home. The house had two bedrooms downstairs and a loft bedroom upstairs. During the time we were living there, I slept upstairs half the time, and the boys stayed upstairs the other half. Our house was located down the street from our church, so the kids and I sometimes walked to choir practice on Saturday afternoons. We even had a garage (something I never had before), so the boys asked to put up a basketball hoop. After getting permission from the landlord, I had some of the guys from work put the hoop up.

Our lives changed completely after that hoop went up; we had an average of ten boys in our backyard at all times! When we got the hoop, Alton was ten; Tony, nine; Emtesha, five; and Mela'nie, two. So having a yard full of kids was pretty typical, but having ten extra boys was, in a word, *loud*! I loved that the boys had so many friends.

Our home was not only close to our church but also closer to my job. Emtesha also had some friends who came over occasionally, and they loved playing with Mela'nie. Things were almost perfect with the exception of not always having enough money to clothe and feed four children.

A few times after picking up the kids from friends or the babysitter, we arrived home to a completely dark house. The first time it happened the kids freaked out, especially when they noticed that the neighbor's lights were still on. How do you explain no lights or TV to your children? Well, I got inventive and told the kids that we were going to pretend we were on a camping trip. So we went to the store and brought some ice for the ice chest to keep the milk and food cold, brought McDonald's home as a special treat. Sometimes if it was warm enough, we roasted hot dogs and made s'mores. Most of their friends wanted to join us for our "camping trips"; they thought it was cool! Thank goodness, the lights didn't stay off more than a day. I could usually borrow some money, until I got paid to get the lights turned back on.

I met a man during my time at Growth whom I became very close with. His name was Shawn; he was working at Milestones Inc., an organization that worked with mentally retarded adults in residential facilities. At first, I hesitated because not only was he Caucasian, but he was also ten years younger than me. The reason that I decided that I couldn't leave him out of my autobiography was because he was the first person I met (since) divorcing both Butch and Joe who truly treated me like a queen. He was very attentive and loving toward me, and he loved my children. After we had been dating for a while, he tried to give me some money to help out with my bills, but I refused; it just didn't feel right accepting money from him. But because he knew I needed it, he would find someplace in the house or my car to hide the money where I would eventually find it. At one point of our "on-again off-again" relationship, Shawn also worked at Growth; this was good and bad at the same time. I liked seeing him every day, but sometimes lines got blurred when it came to our respective positions. Shawn and I even discussed marriage at one time, but that was soon squashed when he found out that his mother was prejudice against African Americans. It was nice to be treated so special after being with my two abusive ex-husbands. Even though we didn't end up together, I will always have fond memories of my time with him.

And because of the way he treated me, I refused to accept anything less after being with Shawn.

In 1988 after I had been working at Growth for four years, I was asked to take the group of mentally ill clients. Most of the staff didn't want to deal with their different attitudes, so when I was asked, my supervisor told me it wasn't an order but a request. I told him I would take the group, and I'm so glad I did. MI people can be different every day. I was used to dealing with clients who could be counted on to be the same every time you saw them.

After working with my group for a week I realized that I needed to touch base with each of them individually before I assigned them a position on the production line. If a client hadn't taken their medication in a few days, they really didn't need to be put on a machine; it's no telling what would happen. Anyway, working with my group was the reason I was offered a position at Janet Wattles Mental Health Center. I had been downtown to the center a few times with my clients when they became unruly, and they could see that I wasn't afraid of dealing with them when it was obvious they hadn't taken their medication. The job offer came with a sizable raise, and I decided to take it. I gave a two-week notice at Growth and said good-bye to my coworkers and my group. Well, when I finished my training at Janet Wattles, I was surprised to find out that the biggest part of my new position was to be a liaison between the mental health center and Growth. It seemed like I was destined to be at Growth, so when I was asked to come back and become the vocational evaluator, I accepted. Since I had only been gone a few months, I was given the same benefit package I had before I left.

I had worked as an evaluator assistant at Goodwill, but it is totally different when you are completely responsible for administering the test, grading them, and writing a report! I kept thinking, *Why did I agree to do this job?* I was sitting in my brand-new huge office with two computers that I didn't really know how to use, test I had never administered by myself, and I felt like running out the door without looking back! I talked to Marge from Goodwill and explained my problem; she told me to come over the next day for lunch, and she would give me some pointers. Marge did more than give me pointers. I left her office with instructions on how to administer all of the test and a mock report for me to follow. Marge was definitely a godsent.

I went back to work with a new determination and decided that I had what it takes to do this job! I found that I really had an aptitude for administering test, and I loved figuring out the statistical part of the evaluations. My reports were delivered on time to the counselors, and I was told that they were very thorough. I continued as an evaluator for the next few years. Because the children kept growing (the nerve of them), their clothes were getting too small, and they started eating more food, especially Emtesha! I have never seen someone as small as she is eat the way she does. Anyway I realized that I needed more income, so I started working part-time at Stepping Stones and at Kenrock Community center. A typical day consisted of getting up around 6:00 a.m., getting the children off to day care or school, and going to work at Growth from 7:30 a.m. to 4:00 p.m. When I got off work I arrived home by 4:15 p.m. and made sure that dinner was started, the children had started or finished their homework, and Alton had everything under control. Then I was off to my job at a Stepping Stones residential facility where I started work at 5:30. My job at Stepping Stones involved assisting the residents with cooking dinner and cleaning the kitchen, taking their evening medications, driving them to activities, and supervising them until they showered and went to bed. I also had to spend the night at the residence (which at the time I didn't get paid for) and get up in the morning with the residence and make sure they ate breakfast, took their meds, and got off to work.

My day at Growth began at seven thirty, so I ran by the house on my way to work and checked on the kids before they left for school. On Tuesday evening I taught mentally retarded adults how to cook simple meals, such as pizza, grilled cheese, pigs in a blanket, and other easy items. I did this three-job routine for around five years. When I share this part of my testimony with someone, they always ask where I found the strength to do everything. My answer is always God. I give all praise and honor to God for giving me what I needed to sustain me during that period of my life. I also thank God for giving me my children: Alton at the time was twelve years old, and he was my right hand during those years. Emtesha learned how to cook, and Mela'nie was a good girl for her brothers. Then there was Tony, he has always been very social, and most days even though he was instructed to stay at home, most evenings he didn't. On one such evening, I found someone to cover for me so I could run home and check on the kids. When I got there, of course, Tony wasn't at home as I expected, and I knew just where he was—at his friend Royce's house. I walked over to Royce's house and found him on his bike talking to one of his running buddies. He looked up and saw me coming, and he looked like he had seen a ghost. I took my belt and beat him all the way to our house! He stayed home for the next few days, but I knew he eventually slipped back out.

Thirty-Four

In October 1991 my whole world changed; I met *my* Oliver! I had been in a small accident in my car and was driving one of the company's vehicles when I first saw Oliver. My grandmother and I lived on the same street, and I passed her house on my way home every day. I had noticed this dark-blue car sitting in her driveway and figured it must be one of her renters. Well, this particular day my grandmother and her renter (Oliver) were out in the front yard raking leaves, so I stopped. I got out and spoke to my grandmother, and she introduced me to Oliver. He looked up from his raking and said hello, and without missing a beat, he went back to his raking. Now I'm not used to being ignored by anyone let alone a man, so I just kind of stared at him and told my grandmother I had to get home and feed the kids, and we said our good-byes. When I got home I called my mother and told her about my encounter with Oliver and told her that I obviously did not make a good impression. I wondered what I had done wrong, I looked in the mirror and noticed that I was looking pretty good, so I couldn't understand his reaction.

For the next month I kept driving by grandmother's house hoping to see Oliver again and maybe make a better impression, but I never saw him, and I noticed that sometimes his car would be there, and sometimes it wouldn't. I figured he worked, but I couldn't make out his hours. Eventually I gave up and decided that it obviously wasn't meant to be. I was working part-time at the local grocery store in the evenings, and one day while I was checking people out at my register, Oliver came through my line. He was dressed like he was going to church; he had on a beautiful blue suit with a white shirt and a beautiful tie. He had on a beautiful off-white over coat and a blue hat. I smelled his cologne first, and I looked up to see who was wearing this wonderful aroma. When I looked up, he smiled and said hello. Then he started asking me questions like, "Do you ever go out to eat?" "What type of food do you eat?" etc. I kept telling him that I really couldn't talk to him because my boss was watching us on camera, and I could lose my job! But he wouldn't leave my lane; he just stood there and smiled at me. Finally, I asked him if he wanted my phone number, and he said yes so, I gave it to him and told him what time I got off work.

That evening when I got home the phone was ringing, and we talked for about three hours before we decided to hang up. I immediately noticed the difference in him; he was nothing like any man I had ever known. The most important difference was that Oliver was a Christian and a minister! Oliver invited me for dinner the next night, and he took me to the Hoffman House! For those of you reading this who have never been to Rockford, Illinois, you probably wouldn't understand the significance of going to the Hoffman House for a first date. Let me just say that the Hoffman House was known for its prime rib. I was so nervous it had been so long since I dated anyone who wore suits like Oliver did, and boy, does he know how to accessorize! On our second date we went to Red Lobsters, another great place to eat, and it also is a far cry from McDonald's or Burger King. Oliver and I talked about the kids and our exes, what we liked doing for fun, and, of course, about church. He also asked me a strange question: "If you had a chance to stop working and stay at home, would you?"

I looked at him like he was crazy and told him no! I loved working and had no intentions of quitting work any time soon! He sat there and smiled at me, and it dawned on me that this may have been a test. I wondered if I passed or not.

During that evening, I told Oliver that I was not happy at my current church because I found it difficult to follow my pastor's way of preaching and his wife's odd behaviors. One example I shared with Oliver was that one evening our church was invited to another church for a night service, our choir was asked to sing, and our pastor was scheduled to preach. I was part of the choir, and all of us were scheduled to meet in one corner of the community room so we could walk in together. We were standing there getting ready to line up when out of the corner of my eye, I saw our first lady coming toward our group, so I just assumed she was coming over to line up with the choir, but when I looked back in her direction, I noticed that she was not wearing our chosen uniform, i.e., black skirts or pants and white shirts; instead, she was wearing the robe of the choir of the church that we were attending! I asked one of the ladies standing near me if she knew why she was in the other choir's robe, and she seemed as astonished as I was. Well, as the evening wore on, I noticed that she did indeed sing with the other church with no explanation from her or our pastor. There were also times that she would sit in our choir stand during the message and call the pastor a liar when he would mention something that he had done during the week.

Since we started seeing each other a few days before Thanksgiving, it was too late for me to change my plans to drive down to my sister Beverly's house in Savoy, Illinois, and my mother and the kids were looking forward to the trip, so we went as planned. I couldn't understand why I was missing a man whom I had just started seeing, but I truly missed him. I told my mother and sister about Oliver, and of course, my mother was very, very impressed—especially because he was a minister! My sister Beverly does not attend church regularly, so she didn't seem to be as impressed until on Thanksgiving Day when Oliver called me and told me that he was thinking about me and wanted to know if I could return earlier than I had planned. Much to the mother and children's dismay, I agreed to return home the following morning, which was Black Friday, the biggest shopping day of the year. Oliver asked if I wanted to go to Milwaukee, Wisconsin, to one of their malls to shop, and of course, I said yes. Do you know any woman who would turn down an invitation to go shopping?

BACK TO THE BEGINNING

The drive up to Milwaukee was a lot of fun; it seemed that we couldn't find enough time to talk about everything. I found out that Oliver was a lot of fun and a great conversationalist. With him being a minister I guess I wanted to know just how crazy I could be without him starting to quote scriptures to me, so I tried some of my raciest things on him, and he just told me that I was a little fast and laughed at me. We had a wonderful time visiting different stores and the numerous venders that set up their booths in the areas between the stores. I found some very unique gifts for my children and other family members. We had dinner, walked around for a while longer, and then decided to return to Rockford. Now I am not usually one to pay attention to the highways that I travel on, but this particular time I was out of town with someone whom I didn't know very well, so I paid special attention to the highways that we were traveling. That was why I was so surprised when we started traveling in a different direction! I thought maybe I was mistaken about the highways we had driven on that afternoon. But soon I realized that I really didn't know where we were; for one thing, all I could see were open fields and farmland when on our way to Milwaukee I noticed stores, businesses, and houses. Finally, I asked Oliver where we were and if we were lost. He looked at me and laughed, saying he was not lost! Well, great, he was not lost but I was. You can imagine the things that went through my mind: He was going to leave me out here in the middle of nowhere, or he was kidnapping me! Finally, Oliver noticed that I was really freaking out, so he told me that he likes to take different ways home, to learn different routes. When it looked like we were returning to civilization, I started to relax. Now that I know Oliver, I'm not surprised when we end up in someplace that looks nothing like where we are supposed to be.

The children weren't so taken with Oliver, because he came across as being very firm and heavy handed. You see, I had raised my children to be dependent on each other and me; they were convinced that we didn't need anyone besides one another and God. Oliver let them know that as long as I wanted him to be there, he wasn't going anywhere! We got into a routine where we all ate dinner together whenever I didn't have to work at one of my part-time jobs. Oliver kept asking me to quit working extra jobs, but I wanted our relationship to be more secure before I quit my other jobs. Oliver told me what his intentions were during our second date; he said he intended to marry me one day! Well, no one had ever said anything like that to me, so I didn't quite know what to do with that piece of news. Oliver also explained to me why he waited a month (after our first encounter) to pursue me. Oliver had been divorced from his first wife for a short time, and he had asked God what his plan was for the rest of his life. God placed it on his heart to contact me after he had prayed and sought God's blessings.

As I mentioned earlier, Oliver lived with my paternal grandmother, and she and I weren't close, but I respected her, and I found out that she respected me also. She had told Oliver about her granddaughter who had four kids, hardworking, and faithfully attending church. Oliver and I hadn't met at that point, but he had met my cousins, and my grandmother told him that I was nothing like them. He said after hearing her description of me he wanted to meet me but only in God's time. Oliver invited me to his church, New Fellowship MB Church, on the east side of Rockford. I told him I would come the following Sunday after I dropped the kids off at our church, Miles Memorial CME Church. When I arrived at New Fellowship, I was immediately astonished to see so many people there whom I knew. Most importantly I saw my good friend Bettye and her family. I was welcomed with open arms, and I felt at home immediately. I visited a few more times and decided I wanted to become a member. I shared my decision with my mother, and she shocked me by asking me to remain at our church until she passed. Now, my mother had been diagnosed with cancer two years before in 1989, but she was attending church and still living alone with an occasional sleepover from one of my children, so this really surprised me. But I felt that I was led to join, and I did the following Sunday, during the month of February in 1992.

My mother died the following June 10, 1992. I guess she knew when it was time for her to go. She just seemed so young at sixty-two, which is my current age. My mother was diagnosed in 1989 with colon cancer. The cancer eventually went to her ovaries, her liver, and her brain. I will never forget the day Mama called me and told me that a truck had stopped and told her to climb aboard, but she told them she couldn't go yet. My mother had told me when I was young that sometimes people will say a train or ship was their mode of transportation from this life, but my mother never liked trucks, so I was surprised when she told me. I asked her if she wanted to get aboard, and she said yes, she did, but she didn't know if everyone would be okay if she left. I assured Mama that everyone would be all right, that she raised us up to be able to take care of ourselves, so we would all be fine. She asked again if I was sure, I knew then that she was concerned about Dennis (her youngest), I assured her that now that Dennis had graduated from law school, he would be fine also.

Mama said, "Okay, the next time the truck comes, I will get on." I caught some grief from some of my relatives asking me why I told Mama she could go. I reminded them that she was ready, and if she stayed, it would only be for everyone else! I appreciated Oliver and the rest of my family for their support, especially when I received a call the morning of my mother's funeral and was told that one of my favorite aunts Carrie V and one of my mother's best friends had passed. I didn't realize just how much time I spent on the phone with my mother until she was gone. Several times I picked up the phone to call her, remembered she was gone, and cried.

Oliver and I spent nearly every day together, and when he had to work at the bakery in the evening, he would come to Growth and pick me up for lunch, or I would take dinner to him at work. I kept wondering when he was going to show his true colors. Oliver worked at Colonial Bakery and had the weirdest hours; sometimes he went to work during the day and sometimes late in the evening. He would tell me as soon as he knew his hours, but I was still skeptical because they weren't consistent. I started driving by his job to see if I spotted his car. I just wanted to make sure he was where he said he was. After we had been seeing each other a few months, we officially became engaged, and I became more secure.

One day out of the blue, Oliver asked if he could start parking his car somewhere else. I asked him what he meant by that question. He replied that he had park in the same spot because he knew I drove by to make sure he was at work! I was so busted. I'm sure if I could have, I would have turned red! He assured me that he understood, and he would do whatever he needed to make sure I felt secure.

On Sunday December 19, 1993, Oliver and I got married. We decided that we didn't want to make a big fuss about the wedding, so we only told a few people. Our best friend Bettye was my matron of honor, and her husband, Jimmie, was Oliver's best man. Oliver and I were both part of the Inspirational Department at New Fellowship, and a few of the members decided that they wanted to give us a dinner after the wedding, so they did a small amount of decorations, and we ordered a cake. I told the people I worked with and some very close friends. After the morning service, our pastor Rev. Charles Threadgill Sr. asked the congregation to remain for a few minutes; there was a surprise that was about to take place. About that time my coworkers and other friends entered the sanctuary. As people started looking around trying to figure out what was going on, Oliver and Reverend Threadgill walked out of pastor's office. Bettye and Jimmie walked in and also stood by Pastor. A few minutes later the pianist played the wedding march, and my oldest son Alton escorted me down the aisle. Oliver and I wore winter white, and Bettye and Jimmie wore purple. It was a beautiful ceremony, and Oliver and I were nervous, but we both agreed Pastor seemed more nervous than we did!

Only three of our children were in attendance, Alton, Emtesha, and Mela'nie; and three of my siblings, Beverly, Charisse, and Dennis. Dennis and my girlfriends Karen and Mary were kind enough to sing during the wedding; it was such a memorable day for all of us. After the wedding we all went downstairs for what we thought were snacks and cake. It ended up being a full-course soulful dinner with all the trimmings. Toward the end of the reception, Oliver and I noticed it was snowing outside, so we decided to get on the road to our honeymoon in St. Louis, Missouri. We spent a few days in St. Louis and then returned home to Rockford, Illinois.

Because we didn't have much of a honeymoon, Oliver and I decided to go on a cruise. We went to see a travel agent who had an office in the North Towne Mall. We finally decided on a seven-day cruise on the SS *Norway*, which is part of the Norwegian Cruise Line. We flew out of Chicago O'Hare International Airport. After spending the night at a park and stay in Rosemont, Illinois, they drove us to the airport. We were able to leave our car in their gated lot, which was also arranged by our travel agent. I didn't realize that going on a cruise would entail so many things; getting certified copies of our birth certificates was not a problem for me, but it certainly was for Oliver. Oliver was delivered by a midwife, and when we received his certified copy, they had the July 28 instead of July 29, which Oliver had always known as his birthday. The only problem having two birthdays created was now Oliver insisted on celebrating both days.

The SS *Norway* is a large ship. In fact, it is so large that we had to take a smaller boat into the ports. Our cruise dates were December 17, 1994, through December 24, 1994, so we were able to experience all of the beautiful decorations and special events that went along with celebrating the holidays. Everyone should go on a cruise at least once during their lifetime. The ship was so large, and there was always something to do, including musicals, gambling, dancing, activities for children, and, of course, swimming in the large pool on the ship. We didn't participate in all of the things on the ship, but we went on shore every time we docked. We went to St. Maarten, St. Thomas, and St. John. I have never seen water so clear, it was breathtaking. We were also to witness a funeral procession, which reminded me of the funerals that I attended in Louisiana. We went to a lot of shops and picked up souvenirs for the kids; however, we really wanted to go up in the mountains where the people on the island actually lived, but that was discouraged.

We shared a table every evening with a couple and their two daughters. The dad was a doctor, and the mom, an attorney, and their daughters were as different as night and day. The youngest of the two teenagers was very adventurous and was constantly getting into something. They were very nice people, and we enjoyed getting to know one another.

The ship had all kinds of shops on board, so we decided to pick out amethyst stones to have rings made when we got home. The thing I enjoyed most was the food, especially the midnight buffets. There was so much food everywhere you look and beautiful ice sculptures. I was surprised that I only got seasick one time I lay down for a few hours and was still able to attend the midnight buffets. Oliver and I also enjoyed the music in the background while we lounged on chases on the top deck and looked at the stars and the moon shining down on the water. You couldn't see land anywhere, and as a person who can't swim, I suppose I should have been a little nervous, but it was so peaceful and romantic that I forgot about not seeing land. I just enjoyed spending time with Oliver.

Thirty-Five

Oliver and I did not have the perfect marriage, but it was close; however, things changed in November 2000. One day while I was driving down East State Street in Rockford, I thought I saw Oliver's son, Oliver Caleb Jr. I circled the block and slowed down when I got to the spot where I had seen him and realized it was him. Now, just seeing Jr. on State Street wasn't the problem; the problem was seeing him in line with other individuals who were waiting to be served at the homeless shelter! After my meetings I drove straight home to tell Oliver what I'd seen. At the time Jr. was nine years old and living with his mother, Linda. I met Jr. shortly after Oliver and I started seeing each other. In fact, I met him when he was around five, and we got along wonderfully. I remember Jr. sitting with me during service when his mother would drop him off at our church. I used to sing in the choir three Sundays out of the month, and people got used to seeing Jr. marching in behind me when the choir entered the choir stand. I always brought snacks and coloring books for him to play with; he loved looking through the small book bag I had just for him to see what I brought for him that Sunday. Anyway I told Oliver about Jr. eating with the homeless, and we tried to contact his mother to find out what was going on. As usual we were not able to reach her, and we decided to try and contact her sisters, Jr.'s aunts. No one seemed to know what the situation was for Linda and Jr.

Well, in about three days we found out exactly what was going on. I was cooking dinner when I heard the doorbell ring. When I answered the door, I found Jr. with a policeman. He asked if I knew Jr., and I told him I did; he was my husband's son. Jr. had told the police that we lived on Central, but he did not know the address, so he wondered if he had found the right house. The policeman said that Linda's neighbor had called and reported that Jr. was once again at her home looking for food, and she didn't know where his mother was. I thanked the policeman and said that I was Jr.'s stepmother, and I would take care of him. From the first day I met Jr., I loved him; he is a very lovable young man. But there was one problem: I didn't count on him living with us permanently!

Let me explain our house had two bedrooms upstairs. One bedroom was used for my office, while the other was our bedroom, and we also had a finished basement where we had an office for Oliver, one large bedroom in which two people could sleep, and another bedroom for one person. Well, when Jr. started living with us, I agreed to give up my office so Jr. could sleep upstairs. I didn't realize at the time how much giving up the room was going to affect me. As you have read throughout my story, I have always tried to do whatever I needed to do for my children. I have tried to put them first always. But one thing I have held on to the whole time I have been raising my children (especially before I met Oliver) was the year 2000. Every time I encountered a setback (which I did constantly), I would say to myself, "This too shall pass." That phrase and remembering the year 2000, which was the year that Mela'nie graduated, I was supposed to be free from sacrificing and raising children!

I think the first time that I realized just how much I was bothered by Jr. moving in was when I pulled into the backyard and saw the light on in what used to be my office! I lost it, I put the car in reverse, and left the house. I couldn't go into my office and do my chill period, around an hour that I would spend listening to music or reading a book, anything to wind down from work. Maybe some of you can't understand my need for quiet time, but working with other people's problems daily, you need to find some time to let their problems go chill and start dealing with whatever is going on at home. I drove around for about forty minutes, and then Oliver called to ask if I was all right because he knew I was usually home by this time. I couldn't tell Oliver what was going through my mind, so I told him I would be home soon, and we could talk.

    I started seeing a therapist regarding my feelings, and I was surprised to learn that I was justified to have these feelings. The therapist told me that I was going through what grandparents raising their children's kids go through. In other words, I had raised my children alone and thought I was done with raising kids and could start living my life now. I felt a little better about the way I was feeling, but it really didn't solve my problem. I talked to Oliver and tried to explain my feelings without him thinking that I was a terrible person and didn't love his son because that wasn't the case. Then other things started happening. Jr. was constantly getting into trouble, he was deliberately doing things we specifically told him not to do, and I know how children can be. His brothers and sisters went through the same phase, but they eventually stopped. Jr. did not! I think that the one thing that topped everything was that Jr. could look right at me and lie. I was generally able to tell when my kids lied, but with Jr., I couldn't. I kept telling myself that Jr. was raised in a different type of home than I raised mine kids. Jr.'s mother had raised him to believe that his father did not care about him and didn't financially take care of him. He was under the assumption that his father was giving all of his time and money to his new wife and children But his mother lied to him. Oliver paid child support each week through the court system. We paid his insurance and also brought things for Oliver for his birthday, clothes for school, and gifts for Christmas, which we wondered if he ever got.

    Oliver and I started arguing about little things that hadn't bothered us before, and it seemed like there was constantly tension in the air. We moved Jr. downstairs to the single room, and that helped some, but it didn't take care of all of our problems. We tried sleeping in different rooms, which actually made things worse instead of better. I eventually found an apartment and moved out. I moved to the other side of town to a two-bedroom place on the third floor.

That was my first time living alone since my second year in college. Emtesha and Mela'nie were both at Western Illinois University, so they weren't home unless it was a weekend or during the holidays. At first I thought it was kind of nice living alone, only caring for myself, not having to worry about cooking or cleaning up after anyone. But eventually I got lonely and started missing Oliver and Jr. Oliver called me the second week after the move and asked if he could come over and see me. I agreed, and we had a very long talk about how we were feeling at that time. We agreed we missed each other, but I wasn't ready to go home. I talked to an attorney about filing for a legal separation or divorce, but he was already representing Oliver in another matter and said he couldn't represent me. I thought maybe this means I should take some more time to think about it. Oliver and I spent the first Christmas apart since we met, the children came over, but it wasn't the same. Oliver and I kept dating, and occasionally he would bring Jr. to visit with him. He asked me to come home, and I told him I would think about it and let him know. We talked a lot on the phone, and I began missing him more, remembering the winter nights I had spent in his arms, and here I was alone when I didn't have to be. I talked to my landlord and told him I needed to move out, and even though I signed a year's lease, he agreed to let me move out, and I agreed to him keeping my deposit.

I returned home to Oliver and Jr. at the end of January 2001. That was the smartest thing I had done since I left in November.

Thirty-Six

One thing that I accomplished while being an evaluator was becoming acquainted with people from other organizations, and in doing so, I started receiving offers for jobs. One such offer came from Stepping Stones Inc., an organization that provided housing, job coaching, among other things for adults with mental illness. I was very interested in the position that they offered me—to run one of their houses and supervise the staff who would be reporting to me. I told the director that I was interested in applying for the position and asked to set up an interview. After interviewing, I was offered the position and told the salary that the job paid. I was astonished; the amount was quite a bit more than I was currently making. There were drawbacks though; at Growth, I was in a position that allowed me to work a lot of overtime, and I was able to work around my kids' schedules. I shared this information with the director, and he assured me that my new position would also be flexible. I asked for a few days to make my decision, and the director agreed.

I spoke with my supervisor Alan the following day, and I told him I was thinking about accepting the offer. He became very upset and said, "You can't leave Growth. We need you here." He asked me to give him some time to talk to our director, and he would get back with me the following day. I was excited about our discussion and shared the news with Oliver and asked what he thought. We agreed that I would seek God's advice about my situation, so I talked to God that evening, and I woke up the next morning feeling relieved. I wasn't sure what my answer would be, but I was reassured that when the time came, I would know.

The next day Alan told me that Growth would meet the amount I was offered by Stepping Stones Inc. I asked what job I would be doing, and he told me to come up with a job title and a list of job duties! I didn't think that I understood him and asked just what he meant. Alan said just what I said, a job title and job duties. So I went back to my office and came up with the title: personal services coordinator. My duties included but not limited to linking clients with various services in the community and attending all special education meetings to determine if students would benefit from becoming part of our program at Growth. I also taught MR clients survival skills, including grooming and hygiene and skills to use in public while shopping, eating at a restaurant, or just interacting with the public. I signed up our clients for Thanksgiving and Christmas baskets. I also taught clients how to make change and place orders. I transported clients and was a replacement supervisor when needed. I stayed busy, and I loved it. Also, because some of my duties involved working after hours, I was able to make as much overtime as I needed to. I thought of myself as an advocate for the clients, a go-between for them as far as dealing with the public.

Some of the staff became upset, saying that I wasn't doing anything or saying I was making money for doing nothing. Alan informed the staff what I was doing and told them to utilize me if they needed assistance with any of their clients. I stayed with this position for around five years until the position of program coordinator became available. I decided to go for it, and I should have been content with what I had. There was no reason for the directors to deny me the position, I had all of the qualifications they mentioned in the advertisement, plus I had years of experience with working at Growth. What I didn't know was that Alan had already picked an individual for the position who didn't work at Growth. Alan didn't bother to share this bit of news with me, so I applied and was given the job. With a catch, I had to continue doing my old job until they found a replacement for me. It was my understanding that I would only have double duty for a couple of weeks, and I figured I could handle that easily. However, I was wrong. The double duty lasted over two months.

I started getting behind in both positions, and the staff started complaining about me not being available for them to ask questions. When Alan came to me with this concern, I reminded him that I was still doing double duty—working both jobs! Finally, after about three months of me trying to balance everything, I was told that I was being replaced for the program coordinator's position with this person whom Alan wanted in the position all along. I was very upset about them bringing in Raven; not only was she from a different agency, but she was also very arrogant and acted as if she knew everything before she even started working.

During this stressful time in my life, my daddy passed on March 17, 2000, after a short illness. My father was my hero; not only did I remind him of his mother, but I was also a daddy's girl from my heart! Daddy had always wanted one of his sons to follow him into his body-and-fender business, but neither of my brothers wanted anything to do with Daddy's business. But I did. I loved hanging out at the shop with my dad and his brother's, my uncles John and Clarence. The Hall men were quite talented; one of them painted, one was a mechanic, and then Daddy did the bodywork. Daddy taught me how to mask cars and how to identify different tools to hand him when I was helping him in the shop. Mostly I worked in the office making calls to customers and trying to find parts. My favorite time was when Daddy and I worked on this one car exclusively; he let me do more work on this car than he ever had. It surprised me, but I loved it. After we finished the car, I was so proud of the work that we had done. My father handed me the keys and told me it was mine!

It was very difficult to watch my father dying. At first, he was in the hospital and then in a nursing home. I was still working, so Oliver was such a huge help to Daddy and I. When Daddy had to move out of his apartment, it was Oliver who helped me. In fact, he got hurt helping me. Oliver was also the one who helped me plan

Daddy's funeral when he passed. Most of my siblings were not close to our father, mostly because of what happened between Daddy and Mama's marriage. Even though my parents had been divorced for several years, they still cared about each other, and I was so happy to learn that the two of them spent time together before Mama died. I know that they wanted to clear the air before either of them passed away.

It was twice as difficult to deal with everything at work and having to bury my dad. So after praying about it, I informed my supervisor and the director that I was talking to an equal-opportunity agency about filing a suit against the company. Some of the board members, my supervisor, and the director set up a meeting with me and agreed that I had been asked to do double duty and was only getting paid for one person. I was able to keep the program coordinator's salary, and I went back to my job of being a personal services coordinator. When Raven started working, she was worse than I imagined! Immediately we clashed, and I knew that one of us had to go. Now being a person of color, I was used to being the one who had to make the compromise, so I decided to start looking for employment elsewhere.

I applied at a couple of agencies until I was contacted by the City of Rockford, Head Start. I was interviewed and was offered the job as a family resource worker. My position included providing case management for thirty-four families through counseling, teaching problem resolution skills, and making referrals to community agencies and service providers. Part of my job involved me visiting parents in the projects, so I did the visits during the day so I could be out by the time it turned dark. I enjoyed working at Head Start until one day about half of us were called into the meeting room and informed that we had been let go. An associate and I looked each other and shrugged our shoulders. I had been contacted by Lutheran Social Services for a possible position, and after the meeting, I called them and set up an appointment for the next day. "When God closes one door, He opens another." Most of the people in that room left there upset, crying and cursing. One of my coworkers asked me why I seemed so calm. I just answered I know God!

I know that it shouldn't take someone else's opinion to make you feel worthy of being treated with respect, but after what I have been through, it certainly helps! It was because of the confidence that I gained that landed me the job at Lutheran Social Services. I went into that interview not knowing a thing about the child services field, but the person interviewing me assumed I did because of my answers. I was offered a position of caseworker working with children in the foster system who were either being returned home to their parent(s) or being placed permanently or adopted into a new family. My job included visiting each child's home and interviewing them even when they were very young. This caused me to become very inventive and learn how to find out if a child at any age is being treated well. I became very good with the parents of the children because I didn't judge them. I reached out to them and tried to work with them instead of against them. I had one parent who had never been taught to clean her house! Her two children were removed because of the terrible condition of their home. The judge told her that if she didn't start keeping her house in better condition, she would permanently lose her kids. Terry (not her real name) was frantic and asked for my help. At first, I told her what products to purchase and tried to show her how to use them. Well, she really didn't know anything about cleaning, so that was useless! I went home and changed clothes, returned, and we cleaned together. It took us several days to get the house in the type of condition that was required for the children to be returned to her.

Once the kids were returned, I spent time with them making sure they knew how to keep their room clean. It was very difficult because by the age of ten and twelve, they should have had years of previous instruction. The mom and I gave the kids incentives to keep their room clean such as an extra hour of outdoor time or extra time watching television. Eventually, all three of them were able to maintain a pretty decent home, and I reported as much to the judge, and the children were permanently returned home to the mom. I kept check on the family once a week to make sure they were maintaining a clean house.

Terry approached me after the children had been returned permanently for two months and asked if she and the children could move to Alabama where her family had some land and her parents had a doublewide trailer for her and the kids to live in. I presented her request to the judge with my personal recommendation, and the judge granted her permission to leave and take her children, but he wanted to have an audience with her first. We were scheduled on the docket the following week, and when she stood in front of the judge, he commended her for her hard work and dedication to keeping her house clean and regaining the custody of her children, and he wished her well in her move to Alabama. It was cases like this one that made the hours of paperwork and visits worth it.

I truly enjoyed my time at Lutheran, and it was because of my position and the work that I had done that I was chosen to be trained as an instructor for PRIDE—Parent Resource for Information, Development, and Education. PRIDE training is mandatory for all new applicants as part of the requirement to become foster parents and or adoptive parents. Part of my job as an instructor was to make a recommendation regarding the appropriateness of the parents in regard to them becoming foster parents. You would be amazed at the number of people who wanted to become foster parents because of the check that they could receive. I really enjoyed teaching PRIDE, and it was a wonderful addition to my résumé.

Part of my job at Lutheran required that I attend a training once a month in Aurora, Illinois. The training was in regard to working with our foster care children with special needs in regard to their education. These meetings were very beneficial because a great number of children in foster care have problems in school. A lot of the kids act out as a way of testing their foster parents or bully other kids because of their insecurities. It was because of my educational background and my work at Lutheran that I applied for the position at NIU. The educational program that hosted the trainings every month was part of NIU. I was offered the job as the assistant to the two instructors of the monthly trainings.

My new job was very much like previous positions that I had in regard to assisting children with educational concerns. I attended special education meetings for children from various agencies in different counties. I did a lot of traveling, and, thank goodness, by this time Oliver wasn't working any more. The bakery closed without notice; thank goodness, Oliver had substantial time, unlike some of his coworkers. Oliver started going out of town with me on almost every trip. No one seemed to mind because Oliver would go somewhere and have coffee and talk to whomever he ran into. One thing about ministers is that they make friends wherever they go, so he looked forward to our little trips. I enjoyed working for NIU, and I had every intention of going back for my master's degree since I could attend classes free!

There was one drawback. I spent a lot of time alone, which didn't bother me at first. I had plenty of work to keep me busy. But as soon I had completed all of the work they assigned me, I had set up for the following months meeting and attended all of the special education meetings, and I started to get bored. I missed the excitement of working on projects with someone and daily interacting with coworkers. I talked to a friend from Illinois Mentor (a child welfare agency) and found out that they were looking for a caseworker, so she suggested that I apply. I applied and was interviewed and submitted my résumé. However, when I received a call a few days later, I was offered a different position: foster parent recruiter/educational liaison.

I gladly accepted the job and gave my two-week notice. I realized later that I should have stayed with NIU. The nonphysical work that I was doing for NIU would have been a welcome relief compared to all of the work I did for Illinois Mentor. Don't get me wrong, I loved working for Illinois Mentor, but I had to eventually leave because of my health. I had to do a lot more traveling than my previous job. It was my job to attend special education meetings for our students such as IEPs, suspensions, expulsions, and manifestation hearings. I was also responsible with coming up with different ways to advertise for foster parents. I designed brochures and billboards and asked different stores and other business if I could put our advertisements in their windows. I did enjoy the once-a-month trips to Chicago, Illinois, for meetings with other Illinois Mentor organizations. We got a lot of good advice and suggestions for doing things differently and getting better results for our agency. I really enjoyed the staff all riding together in the vans; we had so much fun laughing and talking together. Because we had so many different positions we didn't see one another that often. I worked with some of the nicest people in the child welfare business. I saw the caring that the staff displayed to each and every child and parent they encountered. I became good friends with several of the staff during my time at Illinois Mentor, and I loved all of the children and parents.

Thirty-Seven

In February 2008 I noticed that it was difficult to make it through an eight-hour day. It started to become very difficult to get out of bed. I generally woke up in pain, mostly in my knees. And, of course, in the wintertime in Illinois, I had pains in my knees and most other parts of my body. I was almost fifty-six years old, and I kept thinking that I was way too young to be experiencing so many "old folks" symptoms. Most days I forced myself to get up and go to work because I was raised with a very strong work ethic. I also raised my children the same way, so not only was it difficult for me, but I also noticed my children were concerned about my not going to work regularly. I started working partial days, usually six-hour days and making the time up on weekends by doing some of my typing work at home. My supervisor was very understanding and worked with me as long as she could without getting in trouble herself. I noticed that my pain medication was getting stronger to address the increased pain, and the drowsiness was definitely a side effect that limited my production and, of course, my driving.

In April my supervisor and I sat down and talked about my health. She recommended that I come out on disability, and reluctantly I agreed. I could not picture myself not working! I have had a job since I was around five when I sold mud brownies with nuts or when I was twelve and babysat for five children. I couldn't remember a time when I wasn't in school or working or both. I liked the fact that I was able to spend more time with Oliver now that neither one of us was working. We decided to work on the house doing things that we hadn't had time to do before.

In May Oliver and I started talking about moving from Rockford! We had been to Arizona the previous November and in April when our granddaughter Layla was born, so we were thinking about moving to Surprise, Arizona. I think we liked the idea of not having an Illinois winter. Our pastor, family, and friends didn't believe we were actually going to move; they thought we were playing a joke on everyone. However, when we started packing and they saw a For Sale sign in our front yard, the joke was on them. I had been back in Rockford since September 1978 and thought I would always be there. It just seem like the most natural thing to do; after all, my parents spent their whole adult life in Rockford.

There were two states that we were considering: Arizona and Tennessee. I wanted to add Houston to our little list, but Oliver was not in agreement. The decision was made: Arizona or "bust." I went to Arizona in June to find a house for us to rent; not only was Emtesha and her family living in Arizona, but my sister Charisse and brother Melvin and his family also lived there. I found a beautiful three-bedroom home on a corner lot, I was so excited, and it was in walking distance from Emtesha's house!

The drive to Arizona was eventful. I'm so glad we decided to take our time driving there. We stayed in motels when it got dark and continued driving during the day. I loved spending time with just Oliver and I; we spent time getting to know each other again, and I took pictures of everything. Our last stop before Surprise was in Flagstaff, Arizona. We didn't think we needed reservations, but when we couldn't find a decent hotel, we realized that we were wrong. We stopped at one motel that had their vacancy sign lit. We were a little hesitant, but we were both so tired we felt the safest thing to do was stop. Oliver went in to register and got the key. Now I am not a snob, and I didn't grow up with a silver spoon in my mouth, but this room needed to be quarantined! The bed had the dingiest sheets I had ever seen, so we decided to just lie on top of the spread. After looking more closely at the spread, we decided that we could stay awake and drive a little farther toward our destination. Thank goodness, the manager didn't give us any problems when we asked for our money back. We suddenly realized that we were driving around steep mountains! Oliver was so tired, and I couldn't do any night driving at the time, so we decided to drive very *slowly* down the mountains. Have you ever heard of someone getting stopped by the police for driving too slow? The policeman asked if we were okay, because we were only driving ten to fifteen miles an hour! After we explained our dilemma, he said that he understood and to be careful. Thank goodness, we found a decent place to stay about an hour after we parted ways with the policeman.

We arrived in Surprise, Arizona, at around 8:00 a.m., but our house wouldn't be ready until later that day. We decided to sleep for a few hours at Emtesha's house. We were so excited about moving into our new home, we had lived in our home in Rockford since 1994, so this was definitely an adventure. We wanted to start our adventure with all new things, including furniture. So when we had met with the realtor, signed our lease, and got the keys, we decided to go shopping for at least a bed and a refrigerator. We ended up finding almost everything that we needed, we had sold or given away practically everything we had, so shopping for new furniture was part of our new adventure.

Our furniture was scheduled to be delivered the next day, and the things we had shipped were also due the same week. Oliver was really happy with the house I had chosen. I was relieved because it was where we were staying for . . . who knows how long? I noticed that we were living across the street from a field, but I figured, how bad could that be? Well, I found out when the moving van arrived around the same time that the good watermelons had been picked and the bad or rotten ones were left in the field! The guys tried to keep the door closed, but when you are moving furniture, the door is going to be opened more than closed. I started noticing a few flies had come in the house, so I found some newspaper to swat at them, but before I knew it, we had a house full of flies! Oliver told me that this house was in a terrible spot because of the field across the street. I tried to reassure him that they probably won't plant any more once the rotten watermelons disappeared. He reluctantly agreed that maybe it won't be so bad until we started smelling the cabbage that had been planted in the same spot.

Arizona is a desert. I kind of knew that from watching some of the Westerns that were filmed in Arizona. What I hadn't thought about was the dust storms and the rolling tumbleweed and how it might affect my asthma. When the field wasn't being used for planting, the irrigation (water) was not turned on, so as a result, we had a lot of dust on our patio. Everything we put on the patio was always covered with dust no matter how often we wiped it. We also had a beautiful waterfall in the backyard only we never saw the water or the fall; it was broken! Another thing we noticed about Arizona was their so-called grass! It wasn't grass like we knew it; it was more like straw. Our next-door neighbor seemed to be a pretty decent guy until we found out that he raised Dobermans! Our neighbor had four large Dobermans living in his house. Every time we walked around on the left side of our house, the dogs would go crazy! So far our family was the only positive thing that Arizona had to offer.

Oliver and I started changing our sleeping habits; because it was so hot in Arizona, if you didn't need to go outside during the day, you wouldn't. Oliver and I did our grocery shopping around 3:00 a.m., and we went to sleep around 6:00 a.m. and slept until 2:00 or 3:00 p.m. Of course, our children and our friends back in Illinois thought we had lost our minds! We had signed a year's lease, so unless the realtor agreed to let us out of the lease, we were stuck until August 2009! I decided to call the realtor and explain my health concern; she agreed that we could move out early if we would show the house to perspective renters until it was rented. The realtor put our house back on their company's website, and the calls started coming. Now, we aren't messy people, but to keep a house in showing condition at all times is difficult. Finally the house was rented, and we were free to move.

We had been driving around in our neighborhood trying to find a house that wasn't near a field. I was surprised when Oliver stopped in front of a two-story house. I just looked at him like he was crazy until I saw that the house was beautiful, so I could see why it grabbed his attention. However, all I could think about was my poor knees. The landowners lived right next door (not a good thing)! We were walking around the house trying to get a look at least at the backyard. The landlady saw us walking around and offered to let us take a look inside. The house was actually nicer inside than out, and it was so large! We went upstairs and noticed three bedrooms with a bathroom in the master suite and another bathroom at the end of the hall. We both loved the house, and even though there were only two of us, we imagined having our children and grandchildren over for the holidays and decided it would be perfect. We discussed the amount of the rent and deposit and decided we wanted it. The landlady said the house was available immediately, so we agreed on the first of the following month. After hiring the men to move us, we started packing—let me rephrase that, I started packing. Because I have moved so much, I had become an expert packer, and even though we had a three-bedroom house to pack up, I was through in a few days. Oh, Oliver helped some, but mostly he took down beds and other furniture. The move went well with the exception of the amount of the bill at the end of the move. We had agreed on a price, and the bill was about $500 dollars, more than the agreed-upon price. We found out that because the movers had to make two trips (their choice); we were being charged for the extra gas and time. We called the owners and reminded them of our agreement and also mentioned that a friend of ours had helped the movers, and we weren't asking for money to pay him. Finally, after much deliberation we agreed to pay them just $200 more, and since we already had our things, what could they do but accept our offer. We went out and brought more furniture because we now had a living room and a large den along with an office downstairs. We moved in the new house in May, so we decided to have a sixtieth birthday party for Oliver at the end of July.

    We joined Solid Rock Baptist Church while living in our first house, and we had made some wonderful friends from the church, so we decided to invite everyone to the party. We really didn't expect the whole church to come, but that was what happened. It was a good thing we had a friend cater the party for us. We had tons of food, including everything from shrimp to jerk chicken and everything in between. We had so many people it seemed as if as one group left, another group showed up. We had plenty of food; in fact, everyone who wanted to took food home, and we still had plenty left for the following week. People talked about that party for weeks and weeks. We really loved that house until I noticed that my knees were starting to talk to me. Oh, we had some serious arguments, and eventually they won! I told Oliver that we had to think about moving because even though our bedrooms were the only reason we had to climb the stairs, it amazing how many times you forget something upstairs and have to make another trip up that long flight of stairs.

We decided to speak to the landowners, and they agreed to let us out of our lease if we helped the realtor show the house so they could get some new tenants in line before we left. We agreed, but the only problem was that the landlady was very particular about who rented the house. They liked us because we didn't have any kids, so she wanted another couple (that she approved of) who didn't have children and weren't too young. Her stipulations eliminated most of the people who answered the ad. Finally she agreed on a couple who had one toddler and one on the way. Before we started showing the house, the landlords agreed to return our deposit if the house was left in the same condition we found it in. We actually had the house looking better than when we moved in, so of course, we expected our deposit back. Well, when the realtor found out about our arrangement, he argued against it, telling the landlords they didn't have to give us our money back. Obviously her word wasn't her bond because she refused to return our money! You know *God Don't Like Ugly*, so when we heard that the realtor was having some financial and marital problems and our landlord was diagnosed with cancer, we weren't surprised!

We found an apartment complex that we thought was being built for senior citizens and decided to check it out. We met the loveliest young lady when she gave us the tour of the different kinds of apartments, i.e., one, two, and three bedrooms and three floors with no elevator! We decided that we had to have a ground-floor apartment, so we put in an application and were approved. Because the managers were trying to get apartments rented as soon as possible, they offered a two-month free rent special, which really helped us out because we didn't get our deposit. *God is good all the time, and all the time God is good!*

We moved in as soon as the apartment was finished. We found out that the apartments weren't for senior citizens only, but they were classified as luxury apartments, so we assumed that they would carefully screen everyone. Boy, were we wrong; not long after we moved in to our corner apartment situated directly across from the office, pool, and game rooms, we started having daily visits right outside our bedroom windows by the local teenagers. Now Oliver and I like to sleep in, meaning we don't go to sleep until around 5:00 a.m., and we like to sleep until around 2:00 p.m. The local teens had different plans for us; before school started, they started congregating around 10:00 a.m. and seemed to stay there all day! We complained to the office, and they agreed to say something to the teens, but we didn't have much faith in anything they said because the young lady who had given us the tour had left for a better job, and we found out the manager only wanted to get the all the apartments rented so she could return to her home in Houston, Texas!

Oliver and I really liked our apartment, we were the first ones who lived there, and all of the apartments came with a mounted forty-two-inch television! There were a few drawbacks though: the bathrooms didn't have medicine cabinets, of course the noise right outside our windows, people allowing their dogs to crap in our courtyard, and residents allowing outsiders to use their pass keys to our pools and game rooms. We went through the proper channels registering our complaints and were reassured that our concerns would be addressed, but they weren't.

Thirty-Eight

Oliver and I decided to take a vacation and check out Hot Springs Village, Arkansas. I had always told Olive that I didn't want to live in Arkansas, at least not the part I had seen. So far I had been to Camden (Oliver's hometown); they didn't even have a movie theater! El Dorado, Arkansas; Smackover, Arkansas; and Little Rock, Arkansas, were the other places I had visited during are few trips to the South. I didn't mind a short visit to any of these places, but living there, no way! So, I went online and checked out the village because Oliver has a sister who had a house in there and talked about how nice it was. What I saw on the Internet was nice, very nice! So I called and made an appointment to see some rental property with a RE/MAX agent. After speaking to Oliver's brother Raymond and his wife, Diane, about our plans, they invited us to stay with them during our two-week visit. We insisted that two weeks would be a huge inconvenience, but they reassured us that they would enjoy the company.

When Oliver and I arrived in Camden, we insisted on paying for the groceries while we were in town, and the three of us (Oliver, Raymond, and I) went to two grocery stores and stocked up on quite a bit of food. A couple of days later, Oliver and I went to Hot Springs

BACK TO THE BEGINNING

Village for our tour of rental properties. Gary, our agent, had his wife, Jean, take us around; we saw so many houses we had a difficult time trying to remember all of them. We loved several of them and were trying to make up our mind about which one we liked best when Gary called Jean and told her about a house that had just became available. Jean called and got the renter's permission for us to tour the house, and they agreed. We decided immediately that we loved the house on Jardin Lane, which was located in Maderas Gardens, a beautiful little subdivision that even had their own club house! The monthly amount of the rent was almost half of what we were paying in Surprise, Arizona, and it had three bedrooms and two baths, plus the lawn care was covered in the rent. We had made arrangements to stay in one of the rentals for a few days so we had some time to look at other houses if we chose to. We looked at a few other properties, but our minds were made up; 7 Jardin Lane was the perfect house for us! To guarantee that no one else would steal the house, we paid the first month's rent and deposit before we left to return to Camden.

We really enjoyed our visit with our relatives (Oliver also has four sisters who live in Camden) and looked forward to returning to Arkansas to live. In fact, we even drove back up to the village again before we returned to Arizona. This time we took, Raymond and Diane with us so they could see our new home. Oliver and I returned and started packing once again. We had a difficult time getting out of our lease in the apartment complex, but with all of our registered complaints, we felt justified in leaving. We hired a moving company to come and pick everything up and said good-bye to a few neighbors whom we met while we were all complaining at the main office. Everyone we spoke to were talking about leaving as soon as they could, so they were happy for us.

The trip to Arkansas was beautiful, the scenery between Arizona and Arkansas was breathtaking, so I took loads of pictures. We took our time, staying at motels along the way and doing a little sightseeing. When we got back to the village, we had a difficult time finding the east gate in the dark, but we finally got here, and our realtor directed us to our new home. We had brought an air mattress with us and a few necessities to last a couple of days until our things arrived. It was nice putting our things away for a long period of time; in fact, we signed a three-year lease. Our neighbors were some of the nicest people we had ever met. We often met during our evening walks or just getting the mail from the box; they always had a kind word or just a smile.

I loved life in the village, but we were missing one thing: a church home. One Sunday Oliver's sister invited us to the church that she and her husband visit when they stay at their village residence. I was a little hesitant because the church was a Church of God in Christ, and even though Oliver grew up worshiping in that faith, I had always been either Baptist or a CME Methodist. However, I agreed to visit that Sunday. I was pleasantly surprised when I had been in the service for a little while. I noticed that the members were very demonstrative in their worshiping. It had been a long time since I heard individuals speaking in tongue or dancing around the sanctuary; it was invigorating, and the spirit was contagious! After church we had dinner with the pastor and his family along with my in-laws and other church members. I had such a good time, I told Oliver I wanted to come again. Oliver had also enjoyed himself, so we started regularly attending. Soon, I joined the choir, and Oliver began speaking at least once a month.

About a year after we joined, I volunteered to assist with the finances. I had been a financial secretary for a church in Rockford, and I loved working with figures. The pastor and his wife told me that they really appreciate the help because no one else in the church wanted anything to do with money! I took my job very seriously, so I developed a database with everyone's information and the amount of money they put in weekly. I also made the deposits every Monday because there was a branch in the village. I made out the first tax statements that some of the members had ever had, and I also made a financial statement, which was also a first. The members had a lot of questions about the financial statement, and I realized I also had some concerns about where the money was going for different assessments and dues. I questioned why so much of our little church's money was leaving our treasury. I did not agree with some of the answers I received and realized that there were other things that I didn't go along with. After much prayer and discussion, Olive and I decided to leave the church and seek God's direction to another place of worship.

There are many churches in Hot Springs Village and in Hot Springs, Arkansas. We decided to visit a couple of churches in the village, so we went to their services. The services started promptly at 10:00 a.m. and ended promptly at 11:00 a.m. We noticed that the services were very structured and left very little time for the Holy Spirit; in fact I said amen at one service and received many stares! Oliver and I agreed that we didn't like structured services, so we decided to look for a church home in Hot Springs, a church that had more individuals that looked like us! Oliver and I decided to visit Union Baptist Church; we had met the pastor and his wife during a banquet that we attended with St. Phillips. We spent several Sundays at Union, and we really enjoyed ourselves. The pastor, Reverend Jones, and his wife are wonderful people, and he is an awesome speaker. We also enjoyed the associate ministers who we were blessed to hear, and their choir is wonderful! I especially enjoyed watching one of their ministers as he directed the choir! I really thought we were going to become members at Union we even started paying our tithes there; however, God never led us to join their membership.

One Friday Oliver and I were at my beautician Britney Young's shop. I had just finished having my hair done, and my husband was there to pick me up. We were saying good-bye when Britney introduced us to Mrs. Margie Anderson, a very sweet woman. Mrs. Anderson invited Oliver and me to her church Roanoke Baptist in Hot Springs, Arkansas; we asked where her church was and realized that Roanoke was very close to St. Phillips. In fact, we saw it every time that we turned off of Whittington onto Walnut Street. Anyway, Oliver said he remembered another member of Roanoke; Eddie Brown had also invited us to visit. We decided that we would visit Roanoke the following Sunday; we both enjoyed ourselves, especially hearing Pastor Massey. My only concern was not seeing or hearing a choir! I love music, and I was disappointed that they didn't have a choir. I saw a choir stand behind the pulpit, but it was empty! I know that having a choir should not be a deciding factor, but it really meant a lot to me.

The following Sunday we went back to Union but still didn't feel led to join. Oliver suggested that we visit Roanoke again, so I agreed to go, and I am so glad that we did! Our second visit was wonderful, we were able to see Mrs. Anderson again, but this time she was in the choir stand! They had a choir after all. I found out that the music director, Mrs. Massey, goes on vacation one time during the year, and we just happened to attend church one of the two weeks that she was out of town! I loved the choir and instantly felt that I would enjoy singing with them. We were also blessed to see a woman who had been very friendly toward us when we visited before. Rosa and her husband, Andre, Jackson and Katherine Brown have become very good friends of ours along with several other members of Roanoke. Oliver and I both agreed that we wanted to continue visiting Roanoke, and every time we went we enjoyed the services and the members more and more. Oliver was able to spend time with Eddie Brown, the gentleman who had invited him to Roanoke. We prayed and asked God to direct us to where He wanted us to become members; we both wanted a church home.

We started visiting Roanoke Missionary Baptist Church in July 2012, and we became members the first Sunday in November of the same year! We both love being part of Roanoke. I sing in the Gospel Choir and serve with minister's and deacon's wives on first Sundays. We were blessed to become acquainted with Earlene and Charles Scott and their daughter, Valerie Harper. Because the Scotts live here in the village, I generally catch a ride to rehearsal with them, they are very generous people, and I have appreciated them being willing to stop and pick me up, and they refuse to accept any reimbursement for their trouble. I couldn't be happier, I feel so at home at Roanoke, I have made some wonderful friends there, and I have had the opportunity to sing next to a very special friend, Tammie Finney. I am surprised that Sister Massey continues to allow us to sit together because sometimes we get a little loud! I have had the pleasure of getting to know Pastor Massey and Sister Massey; they are wonderful. Pastor Massey is an excellent speaker and a very caring person who cares about all people not just the members of his congregation. Pastor Massey is also the state president of the Baptist Association here in Arkansas; we are so proud of him. Sister Massey and I have become very special friends, and I love her dearly. As musical director she plays for the Gospel, Male Chorus, and Youth Choirs and is very involved with the district's choir. Sister Massey has an awesome voice, and you can tell that she truly believes and lives what she sings about. I guess you can tell that I love my church home and plan on being a member forever!

Thirty-Nine

My sister Charisse asked if she could interview me for one of her college classes because she was writing a paper about abuse. I agreed and shared one of many incidents with her. At the time I had been away from both of my ex-husbands for a while, but I was amazed at how fresh the memories were and how much they still affected me. After we finished, Charisse told me that I should write a book about my life, and I kind of laughed at the thought and dismissed it until I received the same suggestion from Oliver. I started writing this book in 2008 (about six years ago). I know, a long time for one book! The thing is, as I started writing, the memories just came rushing back. I remembered some of the worst times as if they happened the day before! I found it very difficult at times to relive my life, so whenever I started getting too emotional, I walked away and sometimes I wouldn't go back for a few months.

I decided the title after talking to my oldest daughter, Emtesha. I called her with some ideas I was having, and she helped me put my thoughts together. I had previously titled my book *The Look in My Son's Eyes*, because of the anger and pain I saw in my oldest son Alton's eyes whenever his father beat me. But Oliver suggested that I go back to my childhood and write about everything I had experienced as far back as I could remember. He explained that my past would help the reader, and perhaps me, understand some of the choices I made when I was an adult. In the title I stated that my journey started with faith, then pain, and finally blessings, because that is exactly how I see my life. I had a very strong relationship with God when I was a very young child (I joined church and was baptized at five years old). I loved going to church because I always felt so much peace there. As I mentioned earlier, my mother had taken shots so she wouldn't get pregnant, and I came any way. God had a special reason for making sure I was born. I truly believe "the pain" part came into my life right around the time when my parents divorced. And my blessings came into my life when I decided to allow God to order my steps. And the blessings continue each and every day that I am blessed to wake up next to Oliver!

Most people say that Oliver and I are the perfect couple because we show affection for each other all of the time, and they have never seen us when we are not smiling at each other! Oliver is definitely the person that God created just for me, but we are not perfect; no one is. However, we do have one thing that we live by, and it helps; if we have a disagreement, we discuss it with each other and God; He is the only person we invite into our marriage!

I hope that whoever reads my autobiography walks away with some things that I learned from my experiences:

1. Even if you feel that God has walked away from you during the most difficult times in your life, please know that He didn't. He will never leave you nor forsake you as long as you have faith the size of a mustard seed (Hebrews 13:5 and Matthew 17:20).

2. God gives us free will; in other words he allows us to make our own decisions even when He knows it is not the right decision for us. My first two marriages (if I can call them that) were because of choices that I made. I didn't consult God one time about my decision to marry Butch or Joe. Like so many others, I thought I knew what was best for me.

3. You don't have to be someone's girlfriend, woman, or wife in order to be important. You are important just being you, and it's okay to be alone! You should never allow anyone else to determine your worth!

4. *It is never ever okay for someone to hit you!* If someone tells you they only hit you because they love you, they are lying to you! *You don't deliberately hurt someone you love!*

5. Some people say that children who have lived in abusive situations are generally not successful in life. I don't know about everyone else's children, but we have five grown children who are all college graduates, healthy, and happy. I raised my children in church, I didn't send them, I took them, and I participated with them. Remember God is able to do all things but fail!

6. I believe that God has made someone that is just for you! I also feel that sometimes we miss our special someone because we don't allow God to prepare us for them. When we allow God to choose our mate, He will bring us together with a person who will cherish, love, and respect us as much as we deserve. In 2 Corinthians 6:14a, it says, "Do not be unequally yoked together with unbelievers." In other words, don't settle for less; you have the right to be happy!

May God bless and keep each of you!

About the Author

Lauretta L. Thrist has been happily married to her husband Oliver for over 21 years. Lauretta is the proud mother of three sons and two daughters, the grandmother of nine and the great-grandmother of three. She is a proud member of the Roanoke Baptist Church in Hot Springs, AR where she enjoys singing in the gospel choir. While living in Rockford, IL and Surprise, Arizona, Lauretta was a director for the children's department and a Sunday school teacher.

Lauretta graduated from Northern Illinois University in DeKalb, IL with a BS degree in Elementary Education. She worked for 18 years at IL Growth Enterprises in Rockford, IL serving in several positions including evaluating and supervising adults with disabilities. She has also worked in the child welfare system at both Lutheran Social Services and Illinois Mentor as a case worker and as an educational liaison. Lauretta is retired and enjoying spending time with her husband. She loves to travel and would someday like to visit the Holy Land and Paris, France.

CPSIA information can be obtained at www.ICGtesting.com
Printed in the USA
BVOW08s1200170515

400692BV00001B/141/P